STEAMPUNK ACCESSORIES

STEAMPUNK ACCESSORIES

20 Projects to Help you Nail the Style, from goggles to cell phone cases, pocket gauntlets, and jewelry

NICOLA TEDMAN & SARAH SKEATE

BARRON'S

First edition for the United States, its territories and dependencies, and Canada published in 2012 by Barron's Educational Series, Inc.

Copyright © Ivy Press Limited 2012

This book was conceived, designed, and produced by

Ivy Press
210 High Street
Lewes
East Sussex BN7 2NS
United Kingdom
www.ivypress.co.uk.

All inquiries should be addressed to:
Barron's Educational Series, Inc.
250 Wireless Boulevard
Hauppauge, NY 11788
www.barronseduc.com

ISBN: 978-1-4380-0094-7
Library of Congress Control Number: 2012930850

CREATIVE DIRECTOR Peter Bridgewater
PUBLISHER Sophie Collins
EDITORIAL DIRECTOR Tom Kitch
TECHNICAL EDITOR Marie Clayton
SENIOR DESIGNER James Lawrence
DESIGN JC Lanaway
ILLUSTRATORS Peters and Zabransky and John Woodcock
PHOTOGRAPHER James Pike
MODELS Thomas Ardley, Edd Lawrence, Karishma Mehta, Lucy Myles, Emily Owen, and Georgina Wescombe

Printed in China

Color origination by Ivy Press Reprographics

9 8 7 6 5 4 3 2 1

CONTENTS

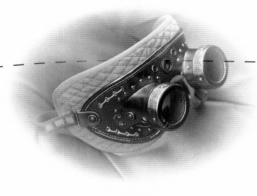

THE PROJECTS

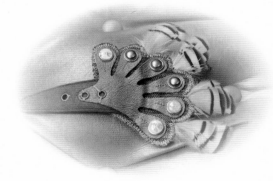

IF, LIKE MOST STEAMPUNK ENTHUSIASTS, you're dedicated to pursuing an exciting hybrid world that has never quite existed, a cross between history and science fiction with a substantial helping of fantasy added in, then you'll already know that attention to detail is key. Maybe you're an aficionado of the works of Jules Verne or Michael Moorcock, maybe you dream of taking trips in a hot-air balloon or a steam train, or maybe the pure individualism of the movement has simply captured your imagination—whichever kind of 'punker you aspire to be, what you wear and how you accessorize your look is an essential part of your image. And although you can now buy a wide variety of steampunk-inspired merchandise, from gauntlets to goggles and jewelry to watch fobs, commercially, nothing will ever equal the individuality of something that you've created yourself, from scratch. This is particularly true if the materials already have a past of their own and you've incorporated them into a brand-new creation—something entirely personal and tailored to your own taste.

Steampunk Accessories offers a complete range of projects guaranteed to meet your need to look just a little different from everyone else. Not only do they offer exemplary steampunk detailing, but they also lend themselves to plenty of customization. You can choose to reproduce exactly what's shown in the picture, or you can change the colors, the materials, or the detailing to work with items you already own, or to complement a planned outfit. As a steampunk fan, you are probably already working outside the box when it comes to the question of your personal image, and everything you'll find here can be made to work in many different ways.

Having the right accessories adds conviction to role play. If you have always wanted to be a fearless adventurer visiting the court of a time-traveling maharajah, you'll find the necessary belt or gauntlets here. Secret compartments and pockets abound, whether they feature in an elaborate bezel ring or an intricate-looking billfold—and no trip, however humdrum, could seem dull when it's undertaken with our exquisitely hand-wrought Zeppelin luggage tags. Your posture will improve when you're wearing a fine hat embellished with our feathered cockade, and our gauntlets come complete with a monocle, so you can stare down the impertinent gaze of passersby who aren't so sure what century you're from.

Above all, these projects are a lot of fun to make. None of the techniques is hard, although some accessories will be much quicker to make than others. And when you've finished, there's something inspiring about knowing that your version is one of a kind and that no one else will ever have another exactly like it.

MATERIALS & TECHNIQUES

FINDING MATERIALS

STEAMPUNK combines vintage with modern, fantasy with reality, and you will need an unusual collection of components to create the look. A good supply of small brass gears, cogs, and decorative keys is essential, along with any other more unusual items you can find to add a personal touch to your creations.

WHERE TO SHOP

An excellent source of gears and cogs is old wristwatches, pocket watches, and clocks of all sizes—broken ones can be picked up for almost nothing at thrift shops or yard sales. Your local watch repairman or secondhand store may also sell you nonfunctioning items or spare parts. If you let them know what you are looking for, they will probably save bits and pieces especially for you. It's also possible to buy basic steampunk cogs and gears on the Internet, particularly on craft sites such as www.etsy.com, which will give you an excellent starting point.

However, to give your projects that unique and personal look, you will also want more unusual components. Old coins, military badges, and medals can also be found at thrift shops and yard sales—look for old or damaged items, or items with missing parts, because these will be less expensive and should have an authentic patina. Ebay is also a good source for all kinds of unusual bits and pieces—look for nonfunctioning items sold for replacement parts.

Jewelry findings, chains, and beads can be found at your local craft or art supply store. There is a wide range of such items available from online stores, too. All kinds of raw (also called natural) and antique brass, gold, or silver charms, pendants, and chains can be bought new, and many online stores now have steampunk sections. Check your local hardware store for brass or bronze nuts, washers, bolts, and chains.

General tips: If you are not sure of a technique, practice it beforehand by making up part of a project, such as the corner of the wallet or a short section of belt, to see how it works.

If an assembled necklace is too short, you can lengthen it by adding extra elements with more jump rings—or shorten a necklace that is too long by removing a section.

Using transfer paper successfully does take practice. Try out the technique on scraps of leather, fabric, or ribbon—if they work well, you can always incorporate them into a project.

The key to having a good range of parts on hand is to keep an eye open for them at all times. If you see an unusual key, a strange button, or anything a little different and appealing, acquire it right away and add it to your stash. You may not have the project for it at the moment, but one day it will be the perfect component—or may even inspire a project of its own.

SUBSTITUTIONS

Finding the pieces to use is all part of the fun—and they do not have to be identical to those used for the projects in this book. Steampunk is supposed to be eclectic and individual, so your finished accessories should be unique instead of exact copies. Don't be afraid to make substitutions; use an old coin instead of a medal—it won't have a hanging loop, but if you need one, you can drill a hole and add a jump ring. The pierced coin used in the necklace on pages 23–26 is a rare find, but you could pierce your own coin or use a cog or circular finding of a similar size instead. As long as something is more or less the right size and shape, and has holes where needed, it will probably work. Buy more coins, keys, medals, beads, pendants, and chains than you need to begin with, so that you can play around to achieve the effect you want.

RECYCLING AND REPAIRING

If a clock, watch, or other item doesn't work and is free or cheap, it's fine to tear it apart to reuse the components. You can also recycle unfashionable or broken jewelry—but first check that the original is not valuable. If the links are not soldered, decorative chains can be taken apart and single links used as unusual jump rings. Short sections of chain are used in several projects in this book, so keep odd lengths for future use. After trips abroad, you may be left with odd coins, which most banks will not change back into your home currency; if they are small denominations, use them as components instead. Some of the projects use scraps of leather or sections of belt; again, thrift shops and yard sales are a good hunting ground. For suitable fabric, ribbon, and trimmings, look for old clothes to cut up and recycle, or oddments left over from other sewing projects.

Simple repairs can make things usable—use a jump ring to add a new clasp or to join lengths of broken chain to achieve the required length. Conceal missing sections by covering with a cog or other decorative addition. Superglue is an acceptable substitute for solder if you need to reattach missing parts without damaging the original.

CLEANING AND AGING

Most old finds will be tarnished or have worn plating, so little needs to be done except to clean them with a soft toothbrush and liquid soap. Use fine wet and dry sandpaper or fine-grade wire wool to rub the highlights and bring out the detail—you can also rub new raw, or natural, brass items to give details a little extra shine.

Bright, new brass items can stand out too much, but you can tarnish them using liver of sulfur or an antiquing rub. At its strongest, liver of sulfur will change the color to black, but you can achieve a range of other colors and effects by using a weaker solution or leaving the piece in the solution for different lengths of time. Antiquing rub comes in a range of colors and finishes and is ideal for adding patina to selected areas.

Using liver of sulfur to add patina

Liver of sulfur is a mixture of chemicals that creates a fast-tarnishing effect on a wide range of metals.

[1] Clean the item thoroughly to remove any wax, polish, or grease, using a solution of baking soda. Mix the liver of sulfur into warm water according to the manufacturer's instructions—the stronger the solution and the hotter the water, the faster it will create a deep patina. Never use boiling water—it causes toxic fumes.

[2] Dip the item in the solution until the desired finish has been achieved, then rinse and dry. You can rub selected areas, if necessary, to highlight the contrast in areas of pattern.

[3] The oxidation will wear off in time and may change color, so protect the surface with a layer of clear lacquer or wax polish.

Using Rub 'n Buff to add patina

Rub 'n Buff is a commercial rub made from carnauba waxes mixed with fine metallic powders and select pigments, available in a range of metallic finishes and in several colors.

[1] Use a small sponge to apply a little Rub 'n Buff over the surface of the metal piece. Let dry slightly.

[2] Buff away some of the polish with a soft cloth until you have achieved the finish you want.

> ✿ **Tip:** Use liver of sulfur in a well-ventilated area because it smells strongly of rotten eggs. Use tweezers to dip the item into the solution to prevent your hands from picking up the smell, too.

TOOLS & TECHNIQUES

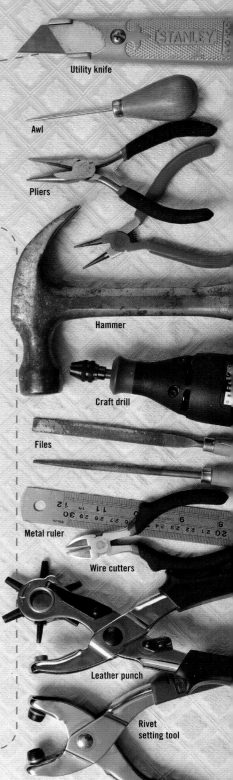

Utility knife

Awl

Pliers

Hammer

Craft drill

Files

Metal ruler

Wire cutters

Leather punch

Rivet setting tool

IF YOU HAVE PRACTICED ANY CRAFT, you probably already have the skills to make most of the projects in this book, but some simple jewelry-making techniques will save you time and give better results. Each of the projects lists the tools you will need, as well as the materials—the most common ones are described here in more detail.

⚙ Useful tools: It's not necessary to buy a lot of expensive tools to begin with, but there are some useful items that you really will need. Many are available from hardware or large craft stores, but you might need to get some from a specialty jewelry supplies store or Internet site.

1 **Wire cutters** For cutting metal chains and snipping off excess wire. The standard type cut the end in a point; the flush cutter type cut the end square.

2 **Utility knife and craft knife** These are available in different sizes, shapes, and styles; choose the one you find most comfortable to use. A utility knife with a retractable blade is the safest. A craft knife is always useful—keep a supply of extra blades handy so that you can easily replace blunt ones. Always protect the work surface underneath when cutting with either type of knife.

3 **Center punch and hammer** Used to create a small indentation in metal so that the drill doesn't slip when you start to drill a hole.

4 **Eyelet setting tool** This squeezes the tabs on the back of the eyelet open to set it in place. There are different types, including a post type that you hit with a hammer.

5 **Rivet setting tool** Used to fit the two halves of a rivet together, in a similar way to setting an eyelet. A simple rivet tool is usually supplied with packages of rivets, but you can also use special pliers that set both rivets and eyelets.

6 **Craft drill and bits** A good selection of drill bits lets you drill small holes in different sizes and in different materials.

7 **Leather punch** This type of punch has a rotating head with several punches in different sizes, so it is versatile and useful for creating small holes, either as decoration or to hold eyelets or rivets. It can be used for materials other than leather, but not metal.

8 **Metal ruler** It can be used for measuring, but a metal ruler is mainly used for cutting against with a knife to guide the blade. Never cut against a plastic or wooden rule because the knife will quickly damage the edge.

9 **Awl** A short, sharp spike set into a wooden handle, used for making small holes through leather and fabric, and to scribe lines.

10 **Metal files** Available in a wide range of sizes and shapes, and useful for removing any burrs left after drilling or cutting.

11 **Round-nose pliers** Used to create loops and rings in wire. The jaws are shaped like a pair of elongated cones so that you can make loops in different sizes.

12 **Flat-nose pliers** The jaws of these are flat with square edges, so they are useful for holding small pieces securely and for creating sharp 90-degree angles. Choose the type without teeth to avoid damaging soft metal or wire.

BASIC JEWELRY-MAKING TECHNIQUES

You will use these basic techniques again and again in the projects. Perfecting them will make your finished pieces look more professional.

Opening and closing a jump ring

Don't open a jump ring by pulling the ends away from each other, because this distorts the shape and it will never revert to a perfect circle. For extra security, add a small dab of superglue to seal the jump ring closed.

[1] Grasp the jump ring with a pair of pliers on each side of the slit. Gently twist the pliers in opposite directions until the slit twists open slightly. To close the jump ring, reverse the twisting action to bring the ends back together neatly.

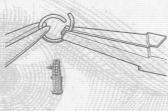

Cutting chain or metal

Cut chain or wire using special wire cutters—not metal snips, which will become damaged. If the chain or wire is thick and heavy, you may need to cut it with a saw. To create the first cut, angle the blade slightly and draw down. File away any rough edges and round off corners with a metal file.

Drilling through metal

Always use new, good-quality drill bits designed for use on metal. (When choosing your drill bit go for one smaller than you think you will need. You can always make the hole larger if necessary but it's much harder to put back material that has been removed.) Drilling into metal can cause swarf (small curls of metal) to be thrown up from the drill tip—always wear safety goggles to protect your eyes. When drilling a small or lightweight item, do not try to hold it in your hand—fix securely in a vice as it will probably move as you begin to drill, which could not only damage your work but also cause injury.

Before you start drilling into metal, mark the drilling point with a fine marker pen, then use a metal center punch and hammer to make a tiny dent into which you can set the drill tip so that it doesn't slip. On smooth, shiny items it may also help to stick on a small square of masking tape and mark the drilling position on it; this will both help to stop the bit slipping and result in a cleaner hole. When you're ready to drill, start drilling slowly and build gradually up to full speed. Finally, remove any burrs with a small, fine metal file.

Using head pins and eyepins

The quickest way to make hanging bead pendants or beaded links to add to a chain is to thread the beads onto a head pin or eyepin. The head pin has a cap at one end, whereas the eyepin has an eye, or loop. Both head pins and eyepins come in various metals and different lengths.

[1] Thread the head pin or eyepin with your chosen beads and bead caps. If the beads are large, start and finish with a tiny bead to make sure that everything sits neatly in line along the wire.

[2] Use wire cutters to trim the excess wire, leaving at least about 5/16 inch (8 mm) above the final bead. Hold the beads in place with your thumb and index finger and use round-nose pliers to bend the wire sharply toward you immediately above the last bead.

[3] Move the round-nose pliers to the top end of the wire and curl the remaining wire away from you and down into a loop—for the eyepin, try to match the size and shape of the eye at the other end.

ADHESIVES & GLUING

A VITAL PART OF CREATING these projects is using adhesives to glue various components together. Poor gluing can ruin an otherwise excellent item, so it's important to be particularly careful at this crucial stage in the process.

PREPARATION

Always make sure that both surfaces to be glued are clean and free of dust and any other loose material, such as burrs left after cutting or drilling. Remove old wax, varnish, or polish—it may react with the adhesive and prevent a strong bond. Gently sand very polished surfaces—including leather—to create a key for the adhesive to grip. If the gluing area is critical, mark the outline with an air-erasable marker pen—this makes a line or mark that gradually fades away when exposed to air. Always use the appropriate adhesive for the materials you want to join.

SPREADING ADHESIVE

When gluing small areas, don't squeeze the adhesive straight from the tube, because this may result in too much adhesive being applied. Instead, squeeze a small amount onto a scrap of paper and then use a small tool, such as a toothpick, to apply the adhesive exactly where you need it. To cover a larger area, use a cotton swab or small sponge to spread the adhesive evenly. A thin, even layer is best; otherwise blobs of adhesive will probably squeeze out the sides of the joint and leave a mark.

When using any type of contact adhesive, spread a thin layer of adhesive on both sides of the joint and let dry. When the two surfaces are pressed together, the bond will be immediate, so be sure to get it right the first time. Excess contact adhesive can usually be rubbed away with a fingertip without marking the surface—but it's worth testing this beforehand on a scrap piece of paper to be sure.

⚙ **Glues:** The projects in this book use four different types of adhesive—the exact type required is listed in the "You will need" section provided for each project.

Two-part epoxy adhesive This type of adhesive begins to bond only when the two parts—resin and hardener—are mixed together in equal quantities. It forms a strong and durable bond at room temperature—the time taken depends on the exact formulation of the adhesive, so check the package instructions if timing is critical. Most two-part epoxy adhesives will bond a wide range of materials, but special formulations are available for bonding metal.

Superglue gel This needs a close-fitting joint and bonds within seconds. It will bond most substances but may not work effectively on some types of plastic. Be careful not to use too much adhesive—a dab or two is usually enough—because it bonds so quickly that it can be difficult to remove any excess before it hardens.

Solvent-based contact adhesive A liquid air-drying adhesive that bonds quickly and permanently on contact pressure. It works on most materials.

Latex-based contact adhesive Similar to solvent-based contact adhesive, but particularly suitable for leather and fabric. Excess adhesive can be rubbed away when dry.

⚙ **Tips:** Always let the adhesive dry for the recommended period of time before proceeding to the next step.

If adhesive squeezes out of a joint, remove it while it is still wet—don't wait for it to dry (unless it is a contact adhesive).

Be ready for accidents—have a damp rag and some warm water ready to clean up spills.

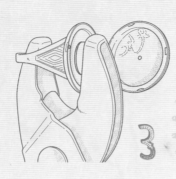

Tips: When setting eyelets, the eyelet-setting tool spreads the tabs on the reverse into a "flower" shape on the back of the work to hold it in place. Make sure that the tabs are evenly spaced: if one side has not opened out fully, the eyelet will not stay firmly in place.

When working on awkward shapes, such as the eyeglass case on page 68, put a post in a vise and set the area of the case that you are working on above it to achieve a firm support behind the eyelet.

EYELETS & RIVETS

Eyelets and rivets are used in many of the projects, either to hold elements in place or as a decorative feature. Jean rivets come in two types—with a flat head or with a nipple head, which has a small centered bump. The nipple-head rivet is more decorative but may be uncomfortable if worn against the skin.

Setting an eyelet or rivet

[1] Punch a hole in the fabric or leather. If working with metal, first place the point of a center punch against the metal and strike the other end with a large hammer to make an indentation in the metal to guide the drill. Drill the hole, filing off any burrs, then push the eyelet or rivet into place.

[2] Although there are many eyelet setting tools available, simple standard setting tools (in different diameters), which include a short metal rod with a special end to be struck with a hammer on a self-healing craft mat or board, will complete all the projects in the book. And they are probably the cheapest option. To set an eyelet, place the tool over the eyelet and tap firmly with a hammer to open out the tabs on the back.

[3] Jean rivets usually come with tools to fix them in place using either a hammer or special variable pliers. Be sure to follow the manufacturer's instructions. To set a rivet, position it where required, then slide the head over the shaft.

Tap with a hammer or squeeze between the jaws of rivet setting pliers. If a smooth rivet is supplied without any tools, place a couple of layers of thick card on each side to hold it in position before setting it.

SEWING

A few projects use sewing. The hand sewing required is basic—perhaps a couple of stitches to hold the odd finding in place—so it should not pose problems, even if you are not confident at sewing. A few projects, such as the goggles on page 110, require machine sewing. For this, you will need a sewing machine capable of heavy-duty sewing. A lightweight machine may not have the power to push the needle through, which will lead to either a broken needle or a damaged machine. Make sure that you can change both the stitch length as required and the pressure of the presser foot to allow for different material thicknesses. At the start and end of a seam, stitch back and forth for a few stitches—this secures the threads and also prevents the line of stitches from unraveling. Use the lines engraved on the needle plate of the machine to help keep your stitches straight.

Tips: Use a fresh needle for each project—blunt needles will lead to uneven stitches and can break.

When sewing across extra-thick areas, stop the machine, then turn the wheel by hand to ease the needle through all the layers.

Stab stitching is a technique of sewing where the needle is held perpendicular to the surface as it is pushed through all the layers, rather than at a shallower angle.

WORKING WITH LEATHER

Several of the projects in this book are made using leather. In most cases, only a small piece is required, so you can buy pieces instead of a whole hide. You may also be able to recycle an old leather jacket, belt, or purse and give it a new lease on life.

CHOOSING LEATHER

Real leather is a natural material, so it may have marks or graining that is part of its charm, although you should try to avoid any pieces with visible damage or thin areas. Leatherette is a form of imitation leather that can look realistic, but it needs special techniques and should not be aged, dyed, or sewn as described here. The most expensive leather is aniline-dyed—the dye sinks into the surface, so the color goes all the way through and the natural surface of the material is still visible. Surface dyeing adds color only to the top surface and also tends to conceal some of the natural beauty of the material.

AGING THE SURFACE

If you are using new leather instead of recycled, you may want to add a patina, a process called "breaking down," which will also make the leather more supple. This can be done by rubbing the surface lightly with sandpaper, and by hammering along a series of folds made in different directions to imitate natural-looking lines of age. Twist and roll the leather as well—this helps to loosen the fibers to make it less stiff and more comfortable to wear. Adding extra color in folds and along edges will also create an impression of age.

MARKING LEATHER

Scribing is a technique of marking a line onto the surface using a sharp point.

DYEING LEATHER

Some leather has a treated surface, which will prevent it from taking a dye, so remove this with a deglazer before you begin—this will be available from the same place you buy the dye. In most cases, it is not possible to make leather lighter in color—you can only make it darker or add a deeper color over the top. If you are trying to match two different items, dye the lighter one to match the darker.

Using leather dye

[1] Apply the leather dye in long, even strokes across the surface, keeping the color even. Let the first coat dry completely before adding more coats. Build up deep colors by applying coats of dye to achieve the desired shade.

[2] Flex the leather several times during the drying process to keep the fibers loose and stop the leather from becoming too stiff. Let the leather dry thoroughly, then buff it with a clean, soft cloth to remove excess dye and produce a polished look.

SEWING LEATHER

When machine sewing leather, use a needle designed specifically for leather. This is shaped like a wedge with a cutting point, which gives it superior piercing power through unyielding fabric. It makes a clean, large hole as it enters the fabric, so it is important to sew accurately because the hole will be permanent. Where possible, tie thread ends instead of backstitching to prevent excessive perforation of the surface.

BEZEL RING

Because this design is based around a locket, you could make an eye-catching necklace instead by using a locket with a hanging loop and threading it onto a leather cord or brass chain instead of mounting it on a ring.

The flower charm used here came from an old earring—recycling parts from broken jewelry is an ideal way of building up a stock of parts to make new pieces.

Use a jean rivet with a flat backing—the nipple-head type will be uncomfortable against your finger.

If you cannot find a suitable brass scarab charm, substitute any small brass insect charm with an opening or a ring from which to hang a jump ring.

✿ YOU WILL NEED

- ✿ Raw brass round or oval locket, about 1 in. (25 mm) diameter
- ✿ Raw brass adjustable ring blank with 15 mm diameter flat face
- ✿ Brass 9 mm flat-head jean rivet
- ✿ Raw brass spoke wheel watch gear, about 1 in. (25 mm) diameter
- ✿ Raw brass leaf spray finding, about 1 in. (25 mm)
- ✿ Raw brass 17 mm scarab charm
- ✿ Raw brass 6 mm bead cap
- ✿ Copper-colored mini craft brad
- ✿ Pair of raw brass clock hands
- ✿ Antique gold 5 mm jump ring
- ✿ Small flower charm
- ✿ Tiny map, photograph, or keepsake to fit locket
- ✿ Center punch and hammer
- ✿ Craft drill
- ✿ ⅛ in. (3 mm) and 1/16 in. (1.5 mm) metal drill bits
- ✿ Wire cutters
- ✿ Small metal file
- ✿ Rivet setting tool
- ✿ Fine-grade wire wool or fine (P600) wet and dry sandpaper
- ✿ Superglue gel
- ✿ 2 pairs of small pliers
- ✿ Two-part epoxy adhesive for metal

CARRY THAT SECRET MAP, personal photograph, or other small keepsake in the hidden compartment of this chunky ring with its stylish period detailing. Raw brass, sometimes also called natural brass, has no plating or lacquer, so it will form an attractive patina in time, which will add to the antique look.

✿ **Note:** Always open a jump ring by holding it on either side of the joint with a pair of pliers and twisting one end away from you. Twist back to close. If you just pull the ends apart, the ring will become distorted and will never return to a perfect circle.

- - - ❀ HOW TO MAKE THE BEZEL RING - - - - - - - - - -

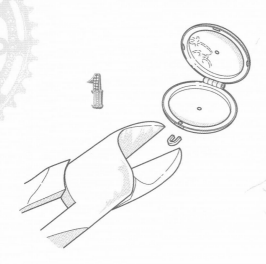

[1] Open the locket and mark the center of the front and back sections on the inside, using the center punch and hammer. Drill a ⅛-inch (3-mm) hole at the mark in the back piece and a ⅟₁₆-inch (1.5-mm) hole at the one in the front part. If there is a hanging loop, snip it off using wire cutters.

[2] Drill a ⅛-inch (3-mm) hole in the center of the face of the ring blank. Smooth off any burrs on both the locket and the ring using a small metal file.

[3] Insert the shaft of the jean rivet through the hole in the back of the locket, from the inside out, and then through the matching hole on the ring blank. Place the rivet head on the end of the shaft, and use the rivet tool or pliers to set the rivet and fasten the locket to the ring.

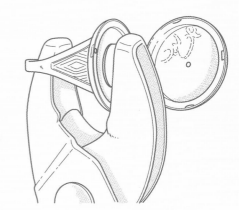

[4] Rub both sides of the spoke wheel watch gear with wire wool or wet and dry sandpaper to prepare the surface. Use dabs of superglue gel to attach the leaf spray and scarab charm to one side of the watch gear, leaving the hole in the middle unblocked. Let the adhesive dry completely. Buff the whole piece with wire wool to enhance the details.

[5] Thread the bead cap onto the arms of the mini craft brad, adding a tiny dab of superglue gel to secure. Slide the clock hands onto the brad, using another tiny dab of superglue on the back of the bead cap to secure. Let dry.

[6] Use superglue gel to stick the assembled watch gear piece onto the front of the locket, lining up the hole in the middle of the watch gear with the hole in the front of the locket. Make sure the head of the scarab and the end of the leaf spray are pointing downward.

[7] Add a couple of dabs of superglue gel to the back of the clock hands. Push the arms of the brad through the hole in the middle of the watch gear and locket. Open out the arms of the brad on the inside of the locket.

[8] Open the jump ring using both pairs of pliers and add the flower charm, then slide one end of the jump ring through a suitable opening in the scarab. Close the jump ring again.

[9] Mix up a small amount of two-part epoxy adhesive and use this to cover and seal the open arms of the brad pin inside the locket. Trim the map or photograph to fit inside the locket, if necessary, and glue in place on the inside.

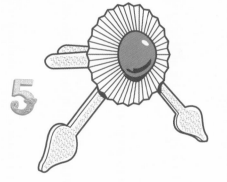

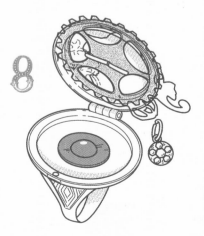

CHANDELIER EARRINGS

- ❋ 3 small halogen capsule bi-pin lightbulbs
- ❋ 5½-in. (14-cm) length of antique brass small ladder chain or similar
- ❋ 8-in. (20-cm) length of antique silver small cable chain or similar
- ❋ 4 antique brass 8 mm jump rings
- ❋ 4 antique brass eyepins
- ❋ 4 metallic gold 4 mm bicone beads
- ❋ 8 antique brass 5 mm flower bead caps
- ❋ 4 clear glass 5 mm faceted round beads
- ❋ 2 antique brass fish hook ear wires
- ❋ 2 raw brass pendant findings
- ❋ 4 antique silver 4 mm jump rings
- ❋ 2 antique brass 5 mm jump rings
- ❋ Fine-grade wire wool or fine (P600) wet and dry sandpaper
- ❋ Wire cutters
- ❋ Flat-nose pliers
- ❋ Round-nose pliers

Any antique finish pendant finding of a similar size can be used, as long as it has three holes on the bottom edge.

Substitute any similar beads if the exact types used here are not available.

THESE DRAMATIC CHANDELIER earrings will give a touch of steampunk to the plainest of outfits; however, if you really want to go for the full look, add the matching necklace on pages 23–26. The exact type of chain used is not important—just make sure that the links are fairly small and the metal has an antique finish.

❋ HOW TO MAKE THE CHANDELIER EARRINGS

[1] Gently sand off the manufacturer's printed markings on the lightbulbs, using wire wool or wet and dry sandpaper. Prepare three lightbulbs because they are easily chipped. Cut both lengths of chain in half.

[2] Using flat-nose pliers in one hand, hold one lightbulb pin near the glass—do not touch the glass because this can cause chips. Using round-nose pliers in your other hand, begin bending over the end of the pin toward the middle. Move the round-nose pliers down the pin a little and bend again until the pin is bent into a curve. Repeat on the other pin, so that the two overlap to make a hanging loop at the top of each lightbulb. Sand off any electroplating that has flaked away from the bent pins.

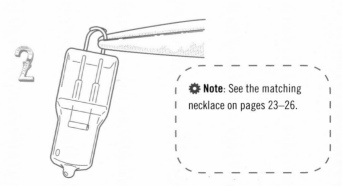

❋ **Note**: See the matching necklace on pages 23–26.

HOW TO MAKE THE CHANDELIER EARRINGS

[3] Open two of the 8 mm jump rings and thread one onto each end of one length of brass ladder chain. Close both jump rings onto a lightbulb loop, being careful not to twist the chain. Repeat steps 2 and 3 with a second lightbulb and length of ladder chain.

[4] Take two of the eyepins and thread one bicone bead, one bead cap, one faceted round bead, and a second bead cap onto each.

[5] Cut off the excess wire and use round-nose pliers to curl the wire end of each eyepin into a loop to match the eye at the other end.

[6] Open each eyepin at the bicone bead end and add an end of one of the lengths of silver cable chain to each. Close the loop again. Repeat steps 4–6 with the remaining two eyepins.

[7] Open the loop at the bottom of each of the ear wires and thread one pendant finding onto each. Close the loop.

[8] Using two of the antique silver 4 mm jump rings, attach the ends of one of the eyepin chains to the outer holes on either side of one of the pendants, being careful not to twist the chain.

[9] Using one of the antique brass 5 mm jump rings, attach the lightbulb loop to the hole in the center of the pendant. Repeat steps 8 and 9 for the other earring.

COG & KEY NECKLACE

T HIS ELEGANT NECKLACE combines vintage and industrial elements into a perfect accessory for the intrepid, sophisticated city girl—and note the matching earrings on pages 20–22. If you can't find a pierced coin and don't want to make one yourself, just drill small holes for the jump rings in any coin or medallion of a similar size.

Any Art Nouveau-style pendant finding of around the same size is suitable for this project—just drill three evenly spaced holes at the bottom if your chosen pendant does not have holes in the required place.

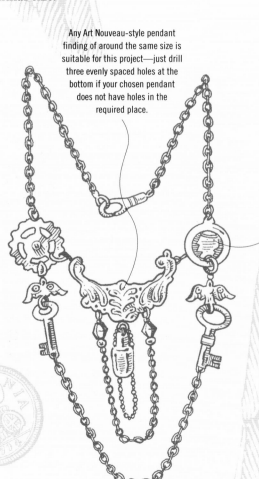

The coin used here is a 1924 British King George V farthing, but any small brass- or copper-colored coin will do as a substitute, such as a typical American penny (make sure it's not a collectible one). Cut out the excess metal by drilling a small hole in the waste area, unfastening and threading the blade of a jeweler's saw through it, then refastening the blade and cutting away the plain metal on each side of the head.

✿ **Note:** See the matching earrings on pages 20–22.

✿ YOU WILL NEED

- ✿ 6 antique brass eyepins
- ✿ Dark-colored seed beads to fit inside each key shaft
- ✿ 2 metal keys, each 1–1¼ in. (25–30 mm) long
- ✿ 1 small halogen capsule bi-pin lightbulb
- ✿ 2¾-in. (7-cm) length of antique brass small ladder chain or similar
- ✿ 4-in. (10-cm) length of antique silver small cable chain or similar
- ✿ 10 antique brass 8 mm jump rings
- ✿ 2 antique copper 5 mm rondelle spacer beads
- ✿ 4 antique brass 5 mm flower bead caps
- ✿ 2 gunmetal or clear glass 5 mm faceted round beads
- ✿ 11 antique brass 5 mm jump rings
- ✿ Raw brass Art Nouveau-style pendant, about 1⅜ x 2 in. (35 x 50 mm)
- ✿ 2 bronze Tibetan-style wing spacer beads
- ✿ 2 metallic silver 4 mm bicone beads
- ✿ 11-in. (28-cm) length of antique brass heavy curb chain
- ✿ Antique brass 8 mm closed jump ring
- ✿ Antique brass 23 mm bag charm clip
- ✿ Raw brass spoke wheel watch gear, about 1 in. (25 mm) diameter
- ✿ Partly pierced brass-colored coin, about ¾ in. (20 mm) diameter
- ✿ 5¼-in. (13-cm) length of antique silver medium cable chain
- ✿ Wire cutters
- ✿ Round-nose pliers
- ✿ Superglue gel
- ✿ Fine-grade wire wool or fine (P600) wet and dry sandpaper
- ✿ Flat-nose pliers
- ✿ Craft drill and bit

HOW TO MAKE THE COG & KEY NECKLACE

[1] Take two of the eyepins and thread onto each one the largest seed beads that will fit inside the shaft of each key. Establish how many beads plus an end loop are required to fill the hole in the key shaft so that just the other loop of the eyepin protrudes at the bottom of the key. Cut off the excess wire and use round-nose pliers to curl the wire end into a loop at the end of the beads.

[2] Dab a small amount of superglue gel onto the top, end, and sides of each beaded eyepin and push one inside each key. Make sure that the eyepin loop at the bottom of each key faces in the same direction as the ring at the head of the key.

[3] Follow steps 1–6 of the earrings on pages 21–22 to make one lightbulb with a chain loop and one length of cable chain with beaded ends. For the necklace, the beaded ends of the eyepins have a copper rondelle bead and a dark glass faceted round bead, but they could be made using the same beads as the earrings, if you prefer.

[4] Using a 5 mm jump ring, attach the lightbulb and chain loop to the middle hole in the bottom of the pendant. Use two 5 mm jump rings to attach the cable chain with beaded ends to suitable holes in the pendant on either side of the lightbulb, being careful not to twist the chain.

[5] Take two more of the eyepins and thread a wing spacer bead onto each, followed by a silver bicone bead. Cut off the excess wire and use round-nose pliers to curl the wire end into a loop.

[6] Using two of the 8 mm jump rings, attach one key to each eyepin loop below the wing spacer beads.

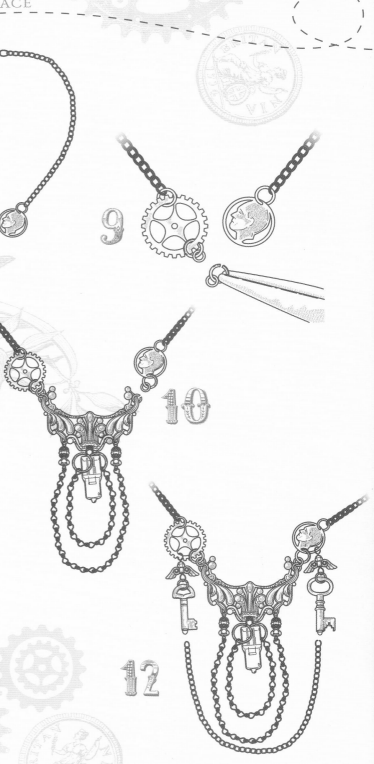

[7] Cut the curb chain in half. Using two 5 mm jump rings, add the 8 mm closed jump ring to one end of one length of chain and the bag charm clip to one end of the other length.

[8] Fasten the bag charm clip onto the closed jump ring and lay the chain down. Using two more 8 mm jump rings, add the spoke wheel watch gear to the free end of the left-hand length of chain. Drill a hole in the top of the pierced coin and add it to the free end of the right-hand length in the same way.

[9] Add an 8 mm jump ring slightly to the right of center at the bottom of the spoke wheel watch gear, then add a 5 mm jump ring onto the 8 mm ring. Repeat on the pierced coin, but this time add the jump rings slightly to the left of center.

[10] Join the necklace by attaching the Art Nouveau-style pendant between the 5 mm jump rings added in step 9, using two more 5 mm jump rings.

[11] Using an 8 mm jump ring through the top loop above a wing spacer bead, attach one key to the bottom of the spoke wheel watch gear. Add the other key to the pierced coin in the same way.

[12] Finish the necklace by attaching the 5¼-inch (13-cm) length of cable chain between the loops at the bottom of each key, using two more 5 mm jump rings. Check that the chain is not twisted before closing the final jump ring.

HIS & HERS BRACELETS

WHAT COULD BE MORE ROMANTIC than matching his & hers bracelets to set the seal on your partnership—particularly if they establish your steampunk credentials at the same time? Of course, you could just make both for yourself instead and wear one on each wrist. The suede and beads in the "her" bracelet can be chosen in colors to offset a favorite outfit, or you could substitute any suitable metal charms.

Both bracelets are worn loose like a bangle, with the fastening above the thumb.

When rubbing the black eyelets back to brass for the "her" bracelet, don't worry about getting all the black off—the idea is just to give a brass highlight to the main part of the eyelet ring.

It is not possible to give an exact measurement for the width of the leather or suede strip, because it will depend on the thickness of the plastic and the thickness of the leather or suede.

> ✿ **Note**: See page 123 for the bracelet template. If you cannot find a sheet of plastic for the bracelet, cut a suitable section of plastic from the side of a laundry detergent bottle.

✿ YOU WILL NEED

MATERIALS FOR HIS BRACELET
- ✿ 1 in. (25 mm) strip from an 8½ x 11 in./A4 sheet of 1/32-in. (1-mm) thick plastic (polypropylene) sheet
- ✿ 6 black 5/16 in. (8 mm) eyelets
- ✿ Piece of brown glove leather, 2 x 8 in. (5 x 20 cm)
- ✿ 16-in. (40-cm) length of antique gold heavy curb chain to fit into 5/16 in. (8 mm) eyelet side by side
- ✿ Small antique brass bar-and-ring toggle clasp
- ✿ 2 antique gold 5 mm jump rings
- ✿ 2 antique gold 8 mm jump rings
- ✿ Blackened metal key, 1¼ in. (30 mm) long

MATERIALS FOR HER BRACELET
- ✿ 1 in. (25 mm) strip from an 8½ x 11 in./A4 sheet of 1/32-in. (1-mm) thick plastic (polypropylene) sheet
- ✿ 6 black 5/16 in. (8 mm) eyelets, rubbed back to brass with fine (P600) wet and dry sandpaper
- ✿ Piece of burgundy suede glove leather, 2 x 8 in. (5 x 20 cm)
- ✿ 18 antique gold head pins
- ✿ 12 metallic gold 8 mm glass bicone beads
- ✿ 12 metallic gold 4 mm glass bicone beads
- ✿ 6 black 8 mm glass bicone beads
- ✿ 12 black 4 mm glass bicone beads

- ✿ 24-in. (60-cm) length of antique gold light curb chain
- ✿ 12 antique gold 5 mm jump rings
- ✿ 8 antique gold 7 mm jump rings
- ✿ 24-in. (60-cm) length of 1/16 in. (1.5 mm) leather cord to match suede
- ✿ 4 antique gold 7 mm box closers
- ✿ Small antique brass bar-and-ring toggle clasp

FOR BOTH BRACELETS
- ✿ Paper and scissors for template
- ✿ Fine permanent marker pen
- ✿ Metal ruler
- ✿ Craft knife and extra blades

- ✿ Small, sharp scissors
- ✿ Leather punch
- ✿ Eyelet setting tool for 5/16 in. (8 mm) eyelets
- ✿ Medium (P80) wet and dry sandpaper
- ✿ Black ballpoint pen
- ✿ Solvent-based contact adhesive
- ✿ Small spatula or sponge to apply adhesive
- ✿ Small hammer
- ✿ Wire cutters
- ✿ Round-nose pliers
- ✿ Flat-nose pliers
- ✿ Masking tape

✿ HOW TO MAKE THE HIS & HERS BRACELETS

BOTH BRACELETS

[1] Scan or trace the bracelet template on page 123 and cut it out. Draw around it onto the plastic using the permanent marker. Cut the straight edges with a metal ruler and craft knife and the round ends with very sharp scissors. Punch out the holes using a suitable punch head or the tool with the eyelet kit.

[2] The holes will probably be slightly too small for the eyelets because of the thickness of the plastic. If necessary, trim them with the craft knife to make them a little larger. Check to make sure all the eyelets fit inside the holes. Sand the plastic well on both sides.

[3] Wrap the leather (for the "his" bracelet) or suede (for the "her" bracelet) around the plastic and measure how wide it needs to be for the edges to butt together down the center. Mark, then trim the leather or suede to width with the metal ruler and craft knife. Use the ballpoint pen to draw a line down the center of the leather on the back.

[4] Spread a very thin layer of adhesive on the back of the leather or suede and on one side of the plastic. Leave until tacky. Using the drawn line as a guide to keep everything straight, glue the plastic along the center of the leather or suede. Wipe a little more adhesive onto the other side of the plastic, making sure it covers all around the holes and edges. Let dry.

[5] Fold over the leather or suede to the marked line at the center of one side; glue one side first, then the other, butting the edges together. Stop at the middle of the final hole at each end.

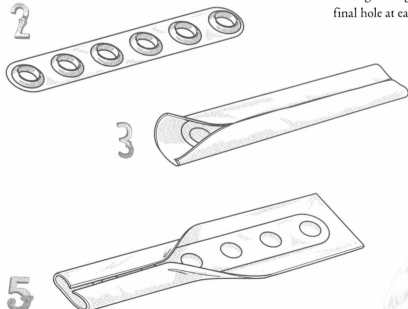

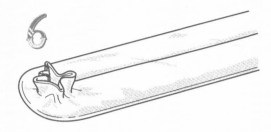

The craft knife blade will become blunt quite quickly when trimming the leather or suede; if so, swap it for a fresh blade immediately.

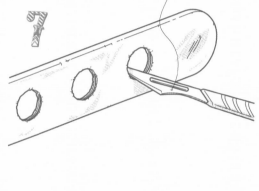

[6] Trim the excess leather or suede to about ⅜ inch (10 mm) at each end. Pull the edge of the leather or suede toward the middle of the final hole, before gluing it down onto the plastic. Work around the hole, trying not to make any creases—it's a good idea to first practice this end hole on a test piece of plastic.

[7] Cut out the center four holes with the craft knife, working first from the back and then from the front. On the back, trim away the excess leather or suede that has been pulled into the two end holes in step 6, holding the craft knife so that the blade is flat to the surface.

[8] Using the hammer, tap the leather or suede down flat and toward the center of the end holes on the back. Cut out each end hole neatly from both sides, using the craft knife. Check to ensure that all the eyelets will still fit into the holes without warping the plastic—trim the hole edges where necessary.

[9] Set the eyelets in the strap—black for the "his" bracelet and black rubbed back to brass for the "her" bracelet.

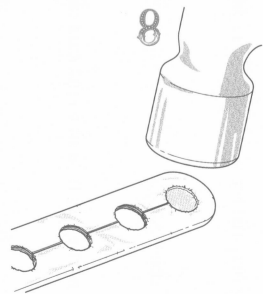

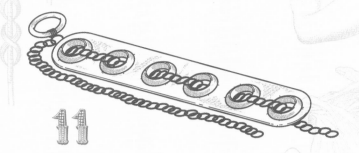

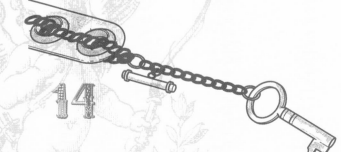

HIS BRACELET

[10] Cut a 14-inch (35-cm) length of the heavy curb chain, find the center, and attach the center link to the ring of the toggle clasp, using a 5 mm jump ring.

[11] Take one strand of the chain under the strap and thread it up from the back through the first eyelet at one end and then in and out through the other eyelets along the length. Be careful to keep the chain flat and not let it twist.

[12] Take the other strand of chain over the top of the strap and into the first eyelet from front to back. Continue threading it in and out of the eyelets, being careful not to twist the chain on itself or twist it around the other chain. Cut both strands of chain a couple of links past the end of the strap.

[13] Take the remaining 2-inch (50-mm) length of curb chain and join the end to the ends of the two strands of chains, using an 8 mm jump ring.

[14] Add the key to the other end of the single length of chain, using the other 8 mm jump ring. Try the bracelet around the wrist and work out where to add the toggle bar—the bracelet is supposed to be slightly loose, with the toggle clasp above the thumb. Add the bar using the remaining 5 mm jump ring.

HOW TO MAKE THE HIS & HERS BRACELETS

HER BRACELET

[15] Take one of the head pins and thread on a gold 8 mm glass bicone bead and a gold 4 mm glass bicone bead. Cut off the excess wire and use round-nose pliers to curl the wire end into a loop. Make another eleven in the same way. Take one of the remaining head pins and thread on a black 8 mm bicone bead and two black 4 mm bicone beads. Cut off the excess and curl the end into a loop as before. Make another five in the same way, using the remaining head pins and beads.

[16] Cut six 1½-inch (40-mm) lengths and six 1¼-inch (35-mm) lengths of the light curb chain. Join together two gold and one black sets of beads, using a 5 mm jump ring. Repeat to make another five sets in the same way. Join together the two different lengths of chain in pairs, one of each length, using the remaining 5 mm jump rings.

[17] Join together one bunch of beads with a pair of chains, using a 7 mm jump ring. Make another five bead charms in the same way, making sure the black beads are between the gold each time.

[18] Cut the leather cord in half and attach two of the ends together by wrapping them with a small piece of masking tape. Starting at the right-hand end of the strap, take the first cord under the strap and up through the first eyelet from the back to the front. Thread both cords through the 7 mm jump ring on top of a bead charm, making sure the chains are behind the beads.

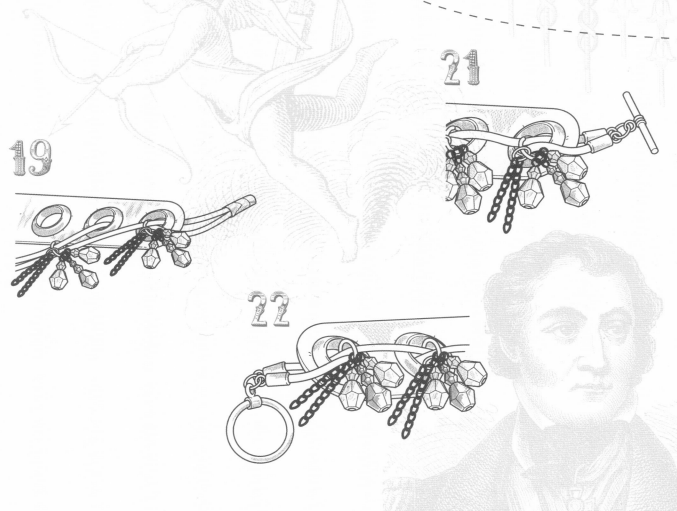

[19] Take the second cord down through the first eyelet from front to back and then back up to the front again through the second eyelet. Thread a second charm onto both cords.

[20] Take the first cord again and thread it through the second eyelet from front to back and then back up to the front again through the third eyelet. Thread another charm onto both cords. Continue in this way, so that both cords are threaded in and out through each eyelet, with a charm threaded on both cords where they cross in the center of the eyelet.

[21] Remove the masking tape and push a box closer onto the end of each length of cord, crimping it in place with the flat-nose pliers. Add the toggle bar to the pair of box closers, using a 7 mm jump ring. Pull the cords from the other end of the strap so that the ends of the box closers are roughly in line with the end of the strap.

[22] At the other end of the bracelet, cut the cord about ½ inch (10 mm) from the end of the strap and add the box closers as in step 21. Add the toggle ring to the pair of box closers, using a 7 mm jump ring.

COGWHEEL BROOCH

❖ YOU WILL NEED

- ❖ 35-in. (88-cm) length of ⅛ in. (3 mm) bronze grosgrain ribbon
- ❖ 17½-in. (44-cm) length of 1 in. (25 mm) navy grosgrain ribbon
- ❖ Bronze sewing thread
- ❖ Small sew-on badge pin
- ❖ Dark brown/bronze topstitching thread
- ❖ Brass pierced clock cog, about 1 in. (25 mm) diameter
- ❖ Brass plain clock cog, about 1½ in. (40 mm) diameter
- ❖ 17–20 small round pearl beads
- ❖ 17 mm raw brass flying bird two-hole connector
- ❖ Small cameo with mount
- ❖ Scissors
- ❖ Sewing machine
- ❖ Iron
- ❖ Pins
- ❖ Hand sewing needle
- ❖ Center punch and hammer
- ❖ Craft drill
- ❖ ¹⁄₁₆ in. (1.5 mm) metal drill bit
- ❖ Beading needle
- ❖ Superglue gel
- ❖ Two-part epoxy adhesive for metal

CAMEOS ARE THE EPITOME of turn-of-the-century style, and here one is combined with authentic-looking medal ribbons and delicate pearl beading. A military award for the sophisticated and socially active woman, perhaps? Pin to a lapel or add a neck ribbon to create a stylish choker that will set off that daring plunge neckline.

> ❖ **Note**: Already-made medal ribbons are available in a range of bright colors and can be purchased by the yard/meter online; however, they can be expensive. Making your own is not only cheaper but also gives you a wider choice when combining colors.

There is not much sewing required for this project, so you could do all the sewing by hand, if you prefer.

Broken pieces of jewelry are an ideal source of pieces to recycle—you could use a section of broken necklace instead of threading on beads for this brooch.

The bronze ribbon is very narrow, so one line of sewing down the center will be enough.

HOW TO MAKE THE COGWHEEL BROOCH

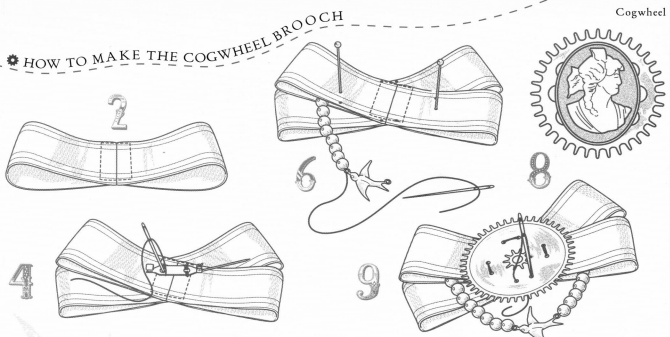

[1] Cut the bronze ribbon in half lengthwise and position one length along each edge of the navy ribbon, ⅛ inch (3 mm) from the edge. Using bronze thread, machine sew the bronze ribbons to the navy one. Iron the ribbon on the reverse, then cut in half widthwise.

[2] Fold each length of ribbon in half, right sides together. Machine sew across ½ inch (10 mm) from the ends. Turn right side out, placing the seam in the center; fold the seam allowance out flat and pin. Sew across the ribbon again on each side of the seam allowance edges.

[3] Place one folded ribbon on top of the other, slightly crossed and with both joining seams facing upward. Pin in place. Sew the layers together in a line down the center.

[4] Sew the small badge pin toward the top of the crossed ribbons, at the center over the seam, using a doubled length of bronze topstitching thread.

[5] Place the smaller cog on top of the larger cog and work out four pairs of stitch holes around the larger cog that will be hidden behind the smaller cog later on. Use the center punch to mark the holes and then drill them.

[6] Place the large cog on the ribbon and mark on each side with a pin. Remove the cog. Thread the beading needle with a length of topstitching thread, knot the end, and bring the needle through from the back of the crossed ribbons and out between the layers of the top ribbon loop at the first point marked with the pin. Thread on about nine of the pearl beads, then take the needle through one hole of the bird connector.

[7] Take the needle back through the row of beads and through the crossed ribbons at the point where you started. Knot the thread on the back, or make a small double stitch to secure, then cut the thread. Thread the needle again and repeat at the second point marked with a pin to add the beads to the other side of the bird connector.

[8] Tack the cameo on top of the small cog with dabs of superglue gel. Turn it over and glue together more securely, using two-part epoxy adhesive through the pierced holes.

[9] Using a doubled length of topstitching thread, sew the large cog in place through all the layers of ribbon. Knot the thread on the back. Using two-part epoxy adhesive, stick the cameo/cog onto the brooch to hide the stitches.

35

If the military badge has a pin fastening on the reverse, you could just pin it to the ribbon and then fold over the ribbon end and sew down.

The watch hangs upside down, so that when you lift it to read the time, it is the right side up.

VICTORIAN TIMEPIECES were never worn on the wrist—gentlemen consulted a pocket watch—but for modern Victorian ladies this watch pin is the answer. A mixture of military styling and decorative dangling chains teamed with a practical chunky watch—what more could the lady of fashion desire?

❋ YOU WILL NEED

- ❋ Copper bead
- ❋ 2 small metallic gold bicone beads
- ❋ Small amber faceted glass bead
- ❋ Antique gold head pin
- ❋ 5–6 lengths of gold-colored chain of different styles
- ❋ Vintage-style watch with spring bars on either side
- ❋ 6-in. (15-cm) length of navy-and-white striped grosgrain ribbon, width the same as spring bar
- ❋ 2 small beads to fit on spring bar (optional)
- ❋ Small brass military badge

- ❋ Dark brown/bronze topstitching thread
- ❋ Raw brass leaf spray finding, about 1 in. (25 mm)
- ❋ Brass pin bar from a medal
- ❋ Antique gold 8 mm jump ring
- ❋ Round-nose pliers
- ❋ Wire cutters
- ❋ Metal ruler
- ❋ Craft drill
- ❋ ¹⁄₁₆ in. (1.5 mm) metal drill bit
- ❋ Small flat metal file
- ❋ Hand sewing needle
- ❋ Scissors

HOW TO MAKE THE LAPEL FOB WATCH

[1] Thread the beads onto the head pin, then cut off the excess wire and use round-nose pliers to curl the wire end into a loop. Cut the lengths of chain into different lengths from 1¼ inches (30 mm) to 2½ inches (65 mm). Thread the head pin and one end of each chain onto the spring bar of the watch, that is next to the twelve on the dial, in ascending order of length. Check to ensure that they hang neatly and are not too crowded or too far apart.

[2] Thread the ribbon through the other spring bar and fold it in half, with the ends together at the top. Check the width; if the ribbon is not quite wide enough, thread a small bead or two onto the spring bar so that the ribbon will not slide from side to side.

[3] Cut any loops off the military badge and drill one centered hole at the top for the jump ring, two stitch holes a little lower down, and another four stitch holes across the bottom. File as necessary. Using a doubled length of bronze topstitching thread, sew the badge onto the ribbon a little way down from the ends, sewing through the holes along the bottom edge of the crown.

[4] Fold the excess ribbon in toward the back of the military badge and baste it down along the fold, taking the stitches through the upper two holes in the military badge. Knot the thread and trim any ends.

[5] Using topstitching thread, sew the leaf spray onto the ribbon through both layers. Attach the badge to the pin bar using the 8 mm jump ring.

> **Note**: Any small leftover lengths of chain can be used for this project; alternatively, substitute short lengths of beading or decorative cord.

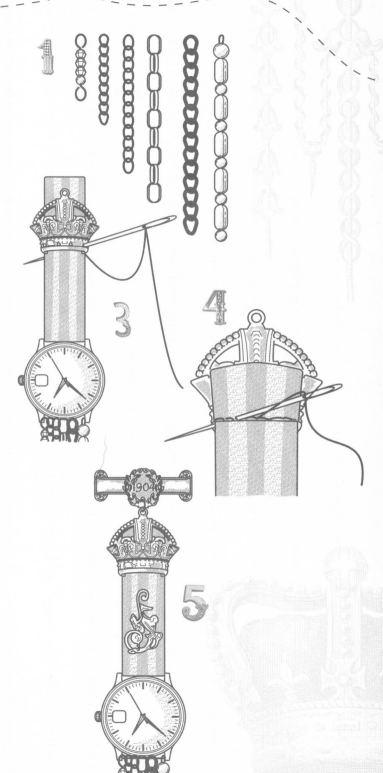

ADVENTURER'S BELT

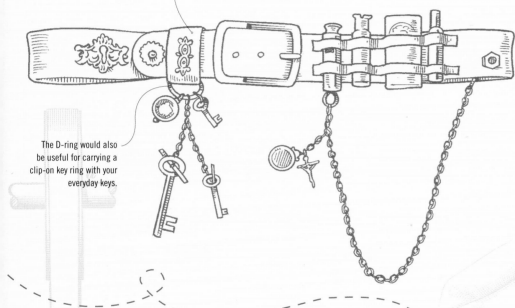

If the belt already has a belt loop, add the D-ring in step 11 by opening it slightly with pliers and sliding it on. Close tightly.

Note: You do not have to use exactly the same items on the belt as shown here—you can choose anything of a similar size and shape. You will need something with an end loop to attach to the other end of the chain.

The D-ring would also be useful for carrying a clip-on key ring with your everyday keys.

YOU WILL NEED

- Heavy brown leather belt with brass buckle
- 22-in. (55-cm) length of ½ in. (10 mm) heavy brown leather strapping
- Black heavy-duty prewaxed thread
- Vintage whistle
- Small glass bottle
- Vintage brass lighter
- Brass bullet casing
- 4 rivets for thick leather (optional)
- Strip of leather for belt loop, 1 in. (25 mm) wide (if belt has no loops)
- Brass D-ring, 1¼ in. (30 mm) wide
- 30 raw brass 12 mm four-hole filigree connectors
- 4 copper mini craft brads
- Raw brass closed wheel watch gear, about 1 in. (25 mm) diameter
- Brass 9 mm flat-head jean rivet
- Decorative brass key plate, about 2 x 1½ in. (50 x 40 mm)
- Bronze topstitching thread
- 24-in. (60-cm) length of antique brass heavy curb chain
- 1–2 antique gold 5 mm jump rings
- Vintage brass cuff link
- 2–3 antique gold 8 mm jump rings
- 3 antique gold heavy sprung hooks
- 2 brass medals
- Small brass crucifix
- 3 metal keys of differing sizes
- 4-in. (10-cm) length of antique brass large etched oval cable chain
- Small antique brass bar-and-ring toggle clasp
- Large antique brass bar-and-ring toggle clasp
- Metal ruler or tape measure
- Utility knife
- Leather dye (optional)
- Leather punch
- Awl
- Heavy-duty hand sewing needle
- Rivet setting tool
- Round-nose pliers

B E READY FOR ANY ADVENTURE with this useful belt, which carries essential gadgets, such as a whistle, keys, and a lighter. Mix and match the items in the loops to suit your lifestyle—a miniature telescope and a pocket compass for serious explorers; a pipe and magnifying glass for sleuths—the possibilities are almost endless.

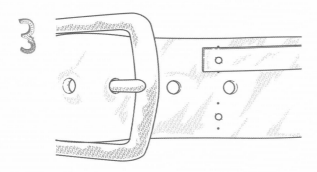

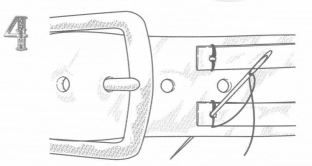

[1] Try on the belt, note which hole the buckle fastens into, and then remove the belt and buckle it again. The tip of the shaped end of the belt should come 3¼ inches (8 cm) after the buckle; if it is longer than this, cut the belt shorter with a utility knife and reshape the end.

[2] Break down the strapping (see page 15) and dye it to match the belt, if necessary. Cut in half and punch a hole near one end of each length, centered on the width, using the smallest hole on the leather punch.

[3] Use the awl to lightly scribe a line across the belt ¾ inch (20 mm) to the right of the buckle. Position the two straps on the belt, lining up the punched holes over the scribed line, and mark through the holes with the awl. Punch out matching holes in the belt. Place each strap back in position, aligning the holes, and mark with the awl on either side of each strap on the vertical scribed line.

[4] Punch stitch holes both sides of each strap through the four awl marks just made, again using the smallest hole on the leather punch. Thread a needle with a doubled length of waxed thread and knot the end. Bring the needle through the hole in the belt and matching hole in the strap from the back, take it over one side of the strap and through a stitch hole, then pass the needle through the loop in the end of the thread and pull tight. Sew the other side, then make another stitch on each side. Knot the thread on the back and trim ends. Repeat for the other strap.

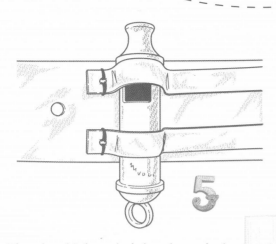

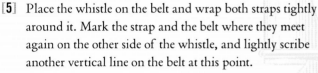

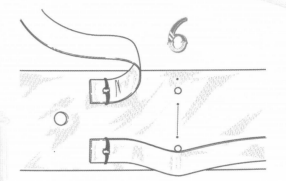

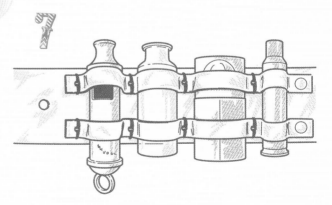

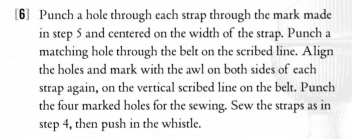

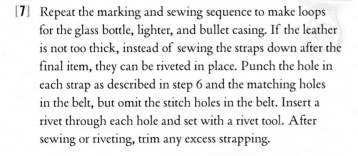

[5] Place the whistle on the belt and wrap both straps tightly around it. Mark the strap and the belt where they meet again on the other side of the whistle, and lightly scribe another vertical line on the belt at this point.

[6] Punch a hole through each strap through the mark made in step 5 and centered on the width of the strap. Punch a matching hole through the belt on the scribed line. Align the holes and mark with the awl on both sides of each strap again, on the vertical scribed line on the belt. Punch the four marked holes for the sewing. Sew the straps as in step 4, then push in the whistle.

[7] Repeat the marking and sewing sequence to make loops for the glass bottle, lighter, and bullet casing. If the leather is not too thick, instead of sewing the straps down after the final item, they can be riveted in place. Punch the hole in each strap as described in step 6 and the matching holes in the belt, but omit the stitch holes in the belt. Insert a rivet through each hole and set with a rivet tool. After sewing or riveting, trim any excess strapping.

[8] If the belt already has a belt loop, skip ahead to step 11. Otherwise work out the length of belt loop required by wrapping the strip of leather around both layers of belt, with the D-ring in place. Trim the strip to length so that the ends will butt up to each other on the back of the belt.

[9] Punch a hole in each end of the belt loop, wrap it around both layers of belt again, and mark the holes on the back of the belt. Unbuckle the belt and punch the holes only in the back layer of the belt. Rivet one end of the belt loop onto the belt. If the rivets will not fit through this thickness, punch stitch holes and sew down one end of the belt loop instead, in the same way as for the straps.

[10] Position the connector in the center of the belt loop front and mark through each corner hole with the awl. Remove the connector and punch the four marked holes through only the belt loop. Attach the connector with four mini craft brads. Rivet or sew down the other end of the belt loop to the belt, remembering to include the D-ring before you secure the end. Buckle the belt again and thread the end through the belt loop.

[11] Position the closed wheel watch gear on the end of the belt and mark the position of the centered hole onto the front layer of the belt, using the awl. Punch the hole. Push the shaft of the jean rivet through the closed wheel watch gear and then into the belt, add the rivet head on the reverse of the belt, then set the rivet.

[12] Place the key plate on the belt and mark through the key plate fixing holes onto the belt using the awl. Punch through the marks to create stitching holes in the belt. Sew on the key plate, using a doubled length of topstitching thread.

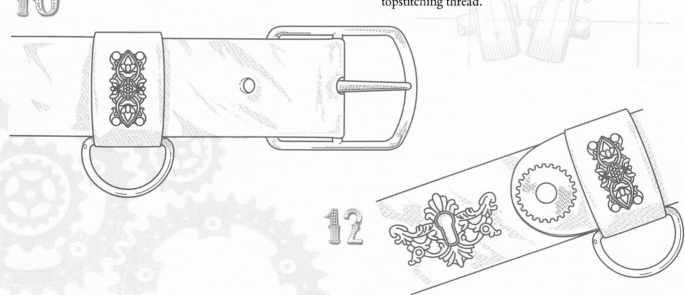

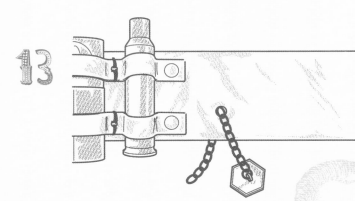

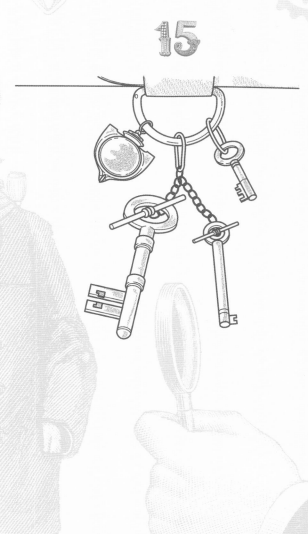

[13] Punch a small hole in the belt just after the bullet casing. Take one end of the curb chain and push a little of it through the hole from the back. Use the small jump ring to attach the vintage cuff link to the end of the chain. Pull the chain back through so that the cuff link lies snugly against the belt front.

[14] Open a bigger jump ring, thread it onto the curb chain 1 inch (25 mm) from the other end, add a sprung hook, and close the jump ring. Attach the sprung hook to the loop of the whistle. Use another big jump ring to add one of the medals and the small crucifix to the end of the curb chain.

[15] Use one or two jump rings, as necessary, to attach the other medal to the D-ring, so that it lies flat. Use a sprung hook to attach the smallest key directly to the D-ring. Open a link at each end of the cable chain with pliers and attach one of the toggle bars to each end. Pass each toggle bar through the hole in the top of the other two keys to attach. Clip a sprung hook off center along the cable chain to attach it to the D-ring, so that the two keys hang at different heights.

FANTASY HAIR CLIPS

Turn heads with these unusual hair clips—ideal for holding back even the most flowing tresses with a touch of steampunk style. The dragonfly and swallow add a touch of fantasy to the design. There are many different versions available, but don't be afraid to substitute any similar small two-hole connector charm.

Note: The coin used here is a British India one-pice coin, but any small brass or copper coin of a similar size and with a central hole would be suitable—although if it is a very old coin, make sure it is not valuable before you attach it to the hair clip.

YOU WILL NEED

- 2 small clock keys
- Gold-colored pocket watch face, about 1¼ in. (30 mm) diameter
- 2 metallic gold 2 in. (50 mm) snap hair clips
- 3¼-in. (8-cm) length of 18 gauge (1 mm) vintage bronze wire
- Brass spoke wheel watch gear, about 1–1¼ in. (25–30 mm) diameter
- Brass-colored coin with hole, about ¾ in. (20 mm) diameter
- 3¼-in. (8-cm) length of 24 gauge (0.5 mm) copper wire
- 6-in. (15-cm) length of antique brass medium curb chain or similar
- Raw brass 19 mm swallow or other flying bird two-hole connector
- Raw brass 19 mm dragonfly two-hole connector
- 6 antique brass 4 mm jump rings
- 6½-in. (16.5-cm) length of antique brass fine cable chain or similar
- 4 antique brass 5 mm jump rings
- Fine permanent marker pen
- Center punch and hammer
- Craft drill
- 1/16 in. (1.5 mm) metal drill bit
- Fine (P600) wet and dry sandpaper
- Superglue gel
- Flat-nose pliers
- Wire cutters
- Two-part epoxy adhesive

If you cannot find a suitable clock key, substitute any small metal key in a bronze or copper color.

When adding the curb chains to the hair clip, make sure that the chain is not twisted before you close the jump rings.

HOW TO MAKE THE FANTASY HAIR CLIPS

[1] Place one of the clock keys across the center of the watch face and mark a dot on each side of the key shaft using a marker pen. Create a guide for the drill by marking each dot using the center punch and hammer, then drill two 1/16-inch (1.5-mm) holes.

✿ HOW TO MAKE THE FANTASY HAIR CLIPS

[2] Place the watch face on the closed end of one of the hair clips, positioning the holes so that the key will sit across the clip at an angle. Mark through the drilled holes with the tip of the marker pen; check to make sure that the marks are not too close to the edges of the clip and adjust, if necessary.

[3] Mark the position of the holes on the hair clip, using the center punch and hammer, then drill 1/16-inch (1.5-mm) holes. Sand any rough edges using fine wet and dry sandpaper.

[4] Glue the key into position between the holes on the watch face, using tiny dabs of superglue gel. Glue the watch face onto the hair clip with another dab of superglue gel, aligning the holes. Thread the length of bronze wire around the key shaft and through the holes to the back.

[5] Twist together the ends of the wire tightly with pliers and cut off any excess. Bend the twisted wire ends as flat as possible to the back of the hair clip.

[6] Glue the spoke wheel watch gear on top of the coin, using a few dabs of superglue gel on the back of the spokes.

[7] Mark, punch, and drill two 1/16-inch (1.5-mm) holes in the second hair clip, positioned to fit inside the center hole in the watch gear. To create a pair of hair clips, the key on this one must be angled in the opposite direction to the first clip, so make sure that the holes are drilled to mirror those in the first clip.

[8] Glue the spoke wheel watch gear and coin to the front of the hair clip using small dabs of superglue gel. Make sure that the two holes drilled in the clip are positioned within the center hole in the watch gear.

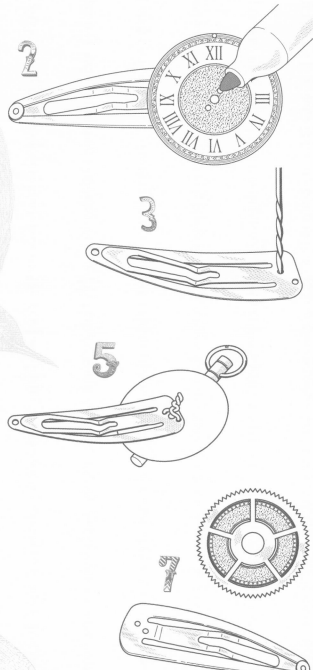

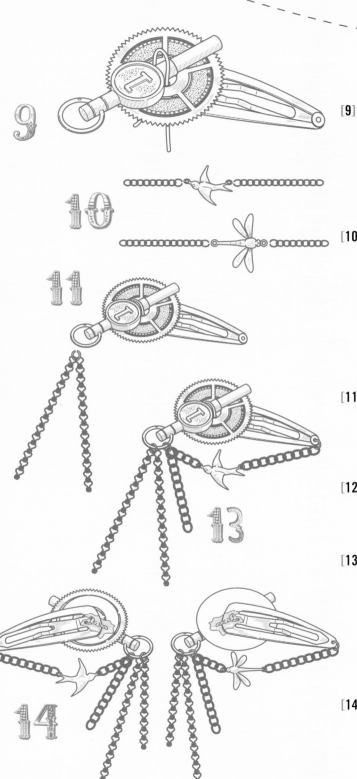

[9] Glue the second key into position between the holes in the clip, using tiny dabs of superglue gel. Thread the length of copper wire around the key and through the holes twice. As before, twist together the wire ends tightly with pliers and cut off any excess. Bend the twisted wire flat to the back of the hair clip.

[10] Cut the curb chain into two pieces 1¾ inches (45 mm) long and two pieces 1¼ inches (30 mm) long. Add the swallow connector to one end of a longer piece of curb chain using a 4 mm jump ring. Use another 4 mm jump ring to add a shorter length of curb chain on the other side of the swallow. Add the dragonfly between the other two pieces of curb chain in the same way, remembering that it should be off center on the opposite side of the swallow to make a pair.

[11] Cut the cable chain in half. Find the center of one length and add a 4 mm jump ring to a link approximately six links to the left of center. Close the jump ring around the ring at the head of one of the clock keys.

[12] Repeat step 11 to add the other length of cable chain to the other hair clip, but this time add the jump ring six links to the right of center.

[13] Take the curb chain with the swallow connector and attach the free end of the shorter length of chain to the hole in the open end of one of the hair clips, using a 5 mm jump ring. Thread the second 5 mm jump ring onto a link almost halfway along the longer length of curb chain from the swallow connector, then add this jump ring to the head of the key.

[14] Repeat step 13 to add the dragonfly curb chain to the other hair clip. Mix up a small amount of two-part epoxy adhesive, and use this to cover and seal the wires and the outside edge of the clip, where it overlaps the back of the watch face or coin.

CANISTER CASE

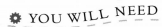

Note: See page 121 for the numbers template. The numbers on the template are already reversed, so there's no need to reverse them to scan—they will transfer the right way onto the ribbon.

If you cannot find a vintage photographic film canister, any small metal canister of about the same size would be fine as a substitute.

You do not have to use numbers—you could print out your name or initials (in reverse) or use a filigree design and transfer that to the ribbon instead.

YOU WILL NEED

- 8½ x 11 in./A4 sheet of iron-on transfer paper (for light-colored fabric)
- 20-in. (50-cm) length of ⅝ in. (15 mm) sage green grosgrain ribbon
- Vintage aluminum 35 mm photographic film canister
- Raw brass four-hole connector, 30 x 10 mm
- 4 silver mini craft brads
- 5 mm filigree bead cap, tapped flat with hammer
- Antique brass head pin
- ½ in. (10 mm) dice
- Metallic silver 4 mm round bead
- Black glass 8 mm bicone bead
- 2 copper 3 mm round beads
- ¾-in. (20-mm) length of antique gold fine cable chain
- 2¼-in. (55-mm) length of antique gold light curb chain
- 3 antique gold eyepins
- Selection of small seed beads in different sizes
- Small silver-colored metal key
- Metallic silver glass 4 mm bicone bead
- Silver Tibetan-style wing spacer bead
- Antique silver 1 in. (25 mm) bag charm clip
- Gunmetal 7 mm jump ring
- 18 gauge (1 mm) craft wire
- Brass 8 mm ring
- 8 mm metal bead with hole big enough for 2 pieces of wire to pass through
- Scissors
- Iron
- Craft drill
- 1⁄16 in. (1.5 mm) metal drill bit
- Round-nose pliers
- Black permanent marker pen
- Awl
- Wire cutters
- Superglue gel
- Two-part epoxy adhesive

Carry your headphones in style with this embellished container made from a genuine vintage pewter-look film canister. It can also be used to carry other small items or small change. The useful bag charm clip means it is easy to hook onto a belt or bag for total portability.

You could substitute a large decorative bead for the dice.

HOW TO MAKE THE CANISTER CASE

[1] Scan the strip of numbers on page 121 and print out onto a piece of iron-on transfer paper. Cut out the strip of numbers, leaving a small border at top and bottom and a larger border at each end.

[2] Iron the transfer paper onto the ribbon, following the manufacturer's instructions. You may have to do this more than once to do it correctly, because the ribbon is thin and absorbent. Let cool, then peel off the backing paper.

HOW TO MAKE THE CANISTER CASE

[3] Take the metal film canister and drill a ⅟₁₆-inch (1.5-mm) hole in the center of both the screw-on lid and the canister.

[4] Using the round-nose pliers, bend the four-hole connector around the canister so that it fits the canister's curve.

[5] Center the connector against the side of the canister and mark through the four holes onto the metal beneath, using the permanent marker. Drill the four marked holes through the canister.

[6] Fold under one end of the ribbon and lay the end over a pair of drilled holes in the side of the canister. Push the awl through the ribbon into the holes to make matching holes in the ribbon.

[7] Place the connector on the canister on top of the ribbon and push two brad fasteners through the holes at one end of the connector, through the ribbon and the canister. Open up the arms of the brads inside the canister.

[8] Pull the ribbon tightly around the canister and fold under as before, so that it just overlaps the other pair of holes. Trim any excess ribbon, then push the awl through the ribbon as before to make matching holes. Secure two more brad fasteners through connector, ribbon, and canister, making sure that the ribbon is tight around the canister.

[9] Thread the bead cap onto a head pin, then thread the pin through the hole in the bottom of the canister from the inside out. Drill a hole through the dice.

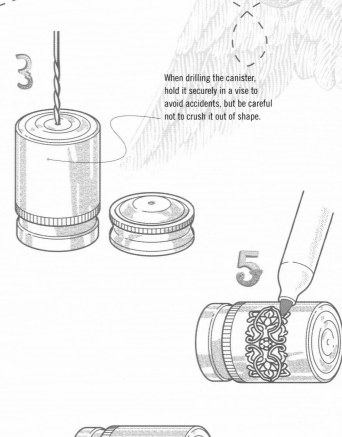

When drilling the canister, hold it securely in a vise to avoid accidents, but be careful not to crush it out of shape.

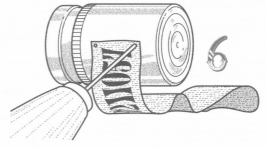

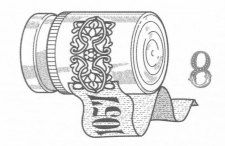

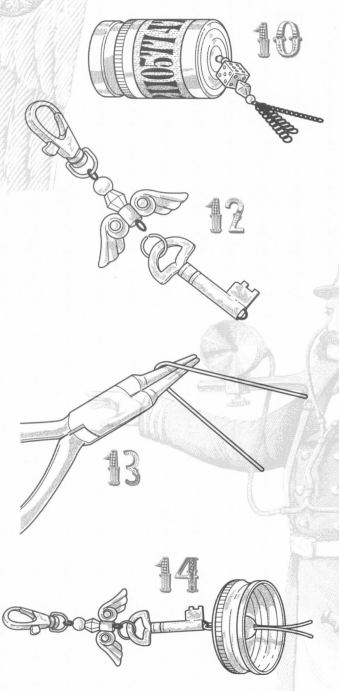

[10] Thread a metallic bead, the dice, a black bicone bead, and a small copper bead onto the end of the head pin below the bottom of the canister. Cut the remaining head pin wire to 5/16 inch (8 mm) and use round-nose pliers to curl the wire end into a loop. Open the loop slightly, and thread on the end of the cable chain and a link to one side of the center on the curb chain.

[11] Thread a few seed beads onto an eyepin until it fits snugly into the shaft of the key. Curl the end of the eyepin into a loop, then secure the beaded eyepin inside the key shaft with superglue gel so that the bottom loop is just protruding from the bottom of the key.

[12] Thread a small copper bead, the silver bicone bead, and the wing spacer bead onto another eyepin. Trim the remaining eyepin wire to 5/16 inch (8 mm) and use round-nose pliers to curl the wire end into a loop. Open the loop at the copper bead end and add it to the bottom of the bag charm clip. Add the key to the other end of the beaded eyepin, using the 7 mm jump ring.

[13] Cut a 3¼-inch (8-cm) length of wire and bend it in half over the smaller end of the round-nose pliers.

[14] Enlarge the hole in the screw-on lid of the canister enough for the two strands of wire to pass through by pushing the awl in from the top. Thread the loop at the bottom of the key onto the wire, then push the two strands of wire through the brass ring and the screw-on lid. Thread the 8 mm metal bead onto both strands of wire inside the lid.

[15] Open out the wires and trim to about 5/16 inch (8 mm). Bend the ends down around the sides of the bead. Mix up some two-part epoxy adhesive and use it to cover the wire ends and the arms of the brads inside the canister to make a smooth surface so that the headphone wires do not catch.

WING & CHAIN FOB

- ❖ 4 small 1¼ in. (30 mm) wing charms
- ❖ 2 brass door keys
- ❖ 12–16 lengths of brass and copper chain in different types and weights, each about 4 in. (10 cm)
- ❖ Brass sewing thimble
- ❖ 18 gauge (1 mm) antique brass wire
- ❖ Copper 3 mm round bead
- ❖ Bronze Tibetan-style wing spacer bead
- ❖ 1¼ in. (30 mm) metal curtain ring
- ❖ 4 antique gold, small sprung hooks
- ❖ 2 pieces of large, etched oval cable chain, each with 3 links
- ❖ 24 gauge (0.5 mm) copper wire
- ❖ 2 brass 5 mm bead caps
- ❖ 8 rose 2 mm rhinestones
- ❖ Black permanent marker pen
- ❖ Craft drill
- ❖ 1/16 in. (1.5 mm) metal drill bit
- ❖ Two-part epoxy adhesive for metal
- ❖ Metal ruler
- ❖ Wire cutters
- ❖ Round-nose pliers
- ❖ Superglue gel
- ❖ Small hammer

The wing charms are attached to the door keys with both glue and wire for extra security.

You can use any selection of brass and copper chains, in different styles and weights.

BECAUSE KEYS are often used in steampunk-style decoration, it seems only fitting that your house keys should be given the steampunk look. Of course, you could just use any miscellaneous keys for a unique piece of jewelry instead.

❖ **Note:** Make sure you keep any added decorative pieces away from the working part of the key.

HOW TO MAKE THE WING & CHAIN FOB

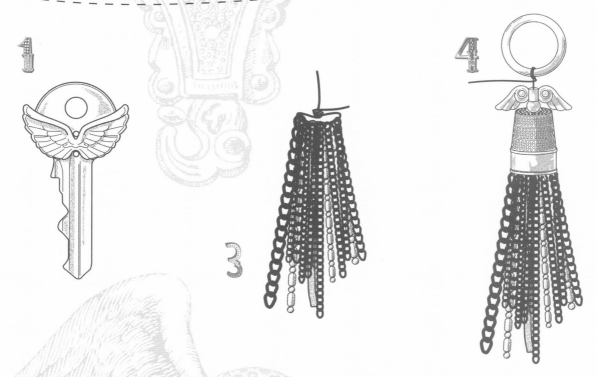

[1] Place a wing charm on each key and mark fitting holes above and below the narrow center section, using the permanent marker. Drill the two holes in each key. Mix up a small amount of two-part epoxy adhesive and use it to glue a wing on each key, being careful to avoid the fitting holes. Let dry. Turn the keys over and glue corresponding wings on this side, too.

[2] Lay out the pieces of different chain and trim, if necessary, so that the lengths vary between 2¾ inches (7 cm) and 4 inches (10 cm). You will need enough strands to comfortably fill the thimble.

[3] Cut an 8-inch (20-cm) length of 18 gauge (1 mm) antique brass wire. Thread the end link of each chain onto one end of the wire, then bend the wire into a U shape, with one end slightly longer than the other. Twist the short end of wire around the longer end three times; don't make the loop holding the chains too tight or they will bunch together and lift outward. Trim the excess wire from only the short end.

[4] Drill a 1/16-inch (1.5-mm) hole in the top of the thimble. Thread the thimble onto the long wire end and push down over the top ends of the bunch of chains. Thread the 3 mm copper bead and wing spacer bead onto the wire after the thimble. Wrap the wire end once around the curtain ring, then wrap it around itself three times below the curtain ring. Cut off the excess wire.

[5] Add a sprung hook to both ends of each of the two lengths of oval cable chain. Hook one end of each piece of chain to the curtain ring.

[6] Cut a 4-inch (10-cm) length of 24 gauge (0.5 mm) copper wire and thread it into the uppermost drilled hole in the key, so that the key sits about halfway along the wire. Thread one end of wire and then the other end through the bottom drilled hole in opposite directions, pull tight, and then bend both ends up toward the top of the key. Cut each end off about ⅛ inch (3 mm) above the top hole. Bend one end at a right angle toward the top hole. Put a tiny drop of superglue gel on the end of the wire and push it into the top hole.

[7] Turn the key over and repeat with the other wire end. Repeat steps 6 and 7 for the other key.

[8] Tap the bead caps flat with the hammer. Glue the bead caps and rhinestones onto the key heads, using tiny dabs of superglue gel.

If you want to make two wrist straps, remember to reverse all the placements so that you have a matching pair.

If the brads securing the ribbon in place are uncomfortable or catch when the wrist corsage is worn, either cover and seal them with two-part epoxy adhesive as described on page 51, or line the inside of the strap with a layer of very thin leather.

❉ YOU WILL NEED

- ❉ 13-in. (32-cm) length of ⅛ in. (3 mm) dark brown leather belting, 1¼ in. (30 mm) wide
- ❉ 4 small Sam Browne brass screw studs
- ❉ 40 in. (1 m) length of ¾ in. (20 mm) turquoise polka-dot grosgrain ribbon
- ❉ Turquoise sewing thread
- ❉ 20-in. (50-cm) length of 18 gauge (1 mm) vintage bronze wire
- ❉ 100 copper-finish 3 mm metal beads
- ❉ 50 metal 4.5 mm rondelle spacer beads
- ❉ 24-in. (60-cm) length of thin, round turquoise leather cord
- ❉ 2 copper nipple-head jean rivets, about 5/16 in. (8 mm) diameter
- ❉ Short length of 24 gauge (0.5 mm) copper wire
- ❉ 2 brass filigree flowers, 1¼–1¾ in. (30–45 mm) diameter, with centered hole
- ❉ 25–30 copper mini craft brads
- ❉ Metal ruler
- ❉ Utility knife
- ❉ Awl
- ❉ Leather punch
- ❉ Slot-head screwdriver
- ❉ Sewing machine
- ❉ Pins
- ❉ Scissors
- ❉ Round-nose pliers
- ❉ Solvent-based contact adhesive
- ❉ Wire cutters
- ❉ Rivet setting tool

A LADY ALWAYS DRESSES bare arms for a formal evening affair, but a wrist corsage of fresh flowers is so predictable. Blaze the way forward with this extravagant steampunk corsage, in which delicate metal flowers are combined with studded leather, beaded wire, and colorful pleated ribbon.

❉ **Note**: Choose any color ribbon you like, but remember to change the color of the leather cord to coordinate.

HOW TO MAKE THE WRIST CORSAGE

[1] Take the length of belting and wrap it around your wrist—it should be slightly loose and overlap by 2 inches (50 mm). Cut it to this length with the metal rule and utility knife.

[2] Scribe two lines parallel to each end of the strap, one at ⅝ in. (15 mm) from the end, and one at 1½ in. (40 mm). At one end punch four holes, two on each scribed line, ⅛ in. (3 mm) in from each long edge. Screw one Sam Browne stud into each hole.

[3] Use a spare piece of leather to establish the correct size "hole with a slit" to fit over the studs. Then make four holes with slits at the other end of the strap to match the studs.

[4] Turn under the raw edge at one end of the ribbon and sew down with the sewing machine, sewing back and forth at each end of the stitches to secure. Measure and mark every ½ inch (10 mm) down one side of the ribbon.

[5] Pleat and pin the ribbon, folding at each ½-inch (10 mm) mark. Do enough pleats to run from the very end of the studded part of the strap to about level with the start of the first slit at the other end. Finish within the nearest pleat before going past this length. Cut off any excess ribbon, turn under the raw edge, and sew in place as before.

[6] Sew the pleats down with a row of stitches 3/16 inch (5 mm) in from one edge. Make a second row of stitches 1/32 inch (1 mm) in from the same edge.

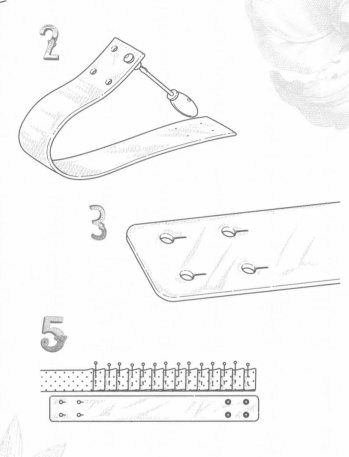

[7] Find the center of the strap and punch a hole for the jean rivet centered across the width but ½ inch (10 mm) from the center toward the studded end. Using the awl to scribe a line ⅛ inch (3 mm) from the top long edge, from the outer stud to where the slits start at the other end. Mark along the line with the awl every ¼ inch (6 mm). Punch a small hole with the awl at each mark.

[8] Along the bottom long edge, scribe two parallel lines ⅛ inch (3 mm) and ¼ inch (6 mm) from the edge, between the studs and the end of the first slit.

[9] Make an awl hole at the studded end of the strap, between the two scribed lines made in step 8. Push one end of the 18 gauge (1 mm) vintage bronze wire through by ½ inch (10 mm) and curl the wire end flat onto the back of the leather using the round-nose pliers.

[10] Push the studs through the matching holes to fasten the strap. Begin to thread beads onto the wire: one round bead, one rondelle bead, then repeat two round, one rondelle in sequence until the beaded wire reaches level with the hole in the center of the strap. Bend the end of the wire at 90 degrees to stop the beads from sliding off. Curve the beaded section of wire around the strap.

[11] Cut a 16-inch (40-cm) length of leather cord and tie a knot 1½ inches (40 mm) from one end. Make two holes in the strap with the awl, one in each of the scribed lines on each side of the beaded wire and level with the middle of the first two round beads. Thread the unknotted end of the cord through from the back, over and between the two round beads on the front, back through the second hole, and pull tight.

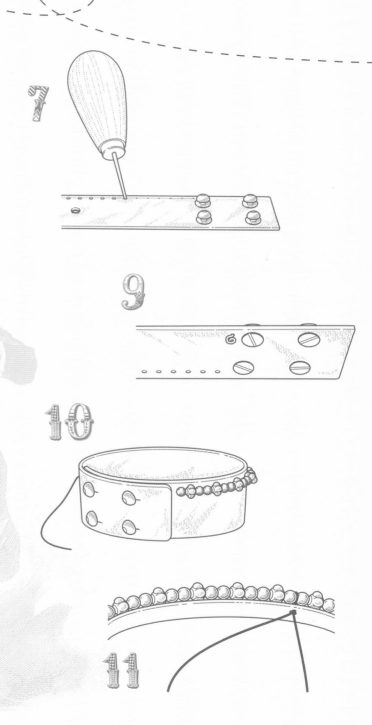

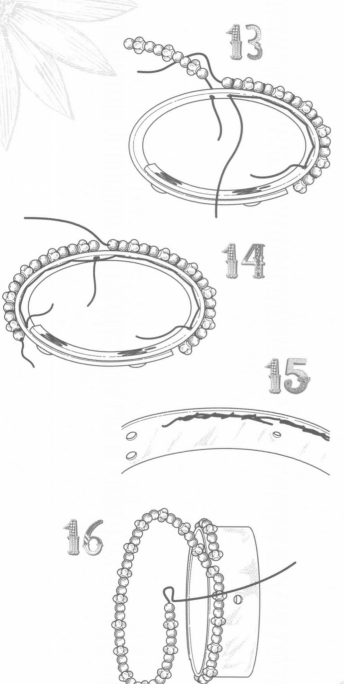

[**12**] Carry on making one stitch at a time between each pair of round beads with the leather cord, as described in the previous step, making the last stitch between the last pair of round beads at the end of the beaded wire. Leave the remaining sewing cord loose for now.

[**13**] Bend the wire off to the side. Take the unused length of leather cord and tie a knot 1½ inches (40 mm) from one end. Make a hole with the awl between the scribed lines, next to the last bead on the beaded wire. Thread the cord through the new hole and begin threading beads on in the same sequence as before until you reach the beginning of the first slit in the strap. Tie a knot in the end of the cord to stop the beads from sliding off.

[**14**] Continuing with the original length of sewing cord, sew the beaded cord down around the edge of the strap in the same way as you did for the beaded wire.

[**15**] Make a hole between the scribed lines near the slits. Undo the knot in the beaded cord and pass this end and the end of the sewing cord through the hole to the back. Knot them together and weave the ends back through the stitches. Trim the ends and glue them to the leather with solvent-based contact adhesive.

[**16**] Slip the strap on your wrist and twist the free end of the wire right around the arm a couple of times to fit. Remove the strap again. Thread beads onto the wire, continuing in the same sequence as before, for about 8¾ inches (22 cm). Bend a loop in the wire.

[17] Thread the wire loop onto the shaft of a jean rivet. Wrap the short length of thin copper wire around the bottom of the wire loop and twist the two ends together to secure the wire loop to the jean rivet. Trim the ends of the twisted wire and curve them around to conceal them inside the rim of the rivet.

[18] Thread one of the flowers onto the shaft of the jean rivet, add the nipple head, and close the rivet with the setting tool to attach the flower in place. Thread more beads onto the wire after the flower, for about another 4 inches (10 cm). Trim the end of the wire to $5/16$ inch (8 mm) and bend a neat finishing loop in the end.

[19] Push in and open up a mini craft brad in the holes along the edge of the strap, omitting a brad about every third or fourth hole equally around the strap. Run a line of solvent-based contact adhesive along the pleated ribbon between the stitches and the edge. Run another line of adhesive on the back of the strap along the row of holes and brads. Leave until tacky. Close the strap up and glue the ribbon trim along the inside edge. Push the awl through each hole without a brad to pierce the ribbon, then push in and open up a mini craft brad in the remaining holes.

[20] Thread the shaft of the second jean rivet through the center hole in the strap from back to front. Add the second flower, then the nipple head of the rivet. Close the rivet with the setting tool.

LUGGAGE TAGS

The thin plastic outer covering of a DVD case is the ideal plastic to use for these luggage tags, because it is easy to cut but still strong. Alternatively, you could use a piece of thick acetate.

YOU WILL NEED

- 1–2 sheets of iron-on transfer paper (for light-colored fabric)
- 2 pieces of beige (or other light color) 1/16 in. (1.5 mm) smooth leather, each 5¼ x 12 in. (13 x 30 cm)
- Sheets of plain paper
- Piece of thin plastic, 3½ x 4¾ in. (9 x 12 cm)
- Dark brown and beige topstitching thread
- Antique brass 8 mm plain rivet
- Copper 9 mm nipple-head jean rivet
- Raw brass spoke wheel watch gear, about 1 in. (25 mm) diameter
- 2 vintage cuff link backs
- 18 gauge (1 mm) craft wire
- 2 pieces of 1/32 in. (1 mm) card stock, each 2¾ x 4½ in. (7 x 11.5 cm)
- Iridescent gold acrylic paint
- Jeweled craft brad
- 7¼-in. (18-cm) length of ball chain
- Ball chain connector
- 2 antique copper 3/16 in. (5 mm) eyelets
- 14-in. (35-cm) length of brown leather cord
- Utility knife
- Metal ruler
- Paper and scissors for template
- Iron
- Sharp scissors
- Solvent-based contact adhesive
- Sewing machine with leather needle and heavy needle options
- Leather punch
- Rivet setting tool
- Craft drill and bit (optional)
- Wire cutters
- Round-nose pliers
- Two-part epoxy adhesive
- Black ballpoint pen
- Small hammer
- Latex-based contact adhesive
- Fine paintbrush
- Eyelet setting tool for 3/16 in. (5 mm) eyelets

LUGGAGE IS ESSENTIAL for every serious traveler, whether your journey is on a Zeppelin, steam train, or automobile, and whether it is a short trip or an epic trek across the globe. Give your luggage a genuine sense of period style by adding these eye-catching leather tags.

Note: See page 122 for the luggage tags templates.

HOW TO MAKE THE LUGGAGE TAGS

Note: If you don't have a scanner, you may be able to get the images copied onto the image transfer paper at a printing or photocopying store.

[1] Scan the oval frame and Zeppelin images on page 123 and print out onto sheets of iron-on transfer paper. The images are already flipped, so they will set the right way when ironed on. Cut out the rectangles using a utility knife and metal ruler, leaving a narrow white border.

[2] Scan or trace the luggage tag outline template on page 122 and cut it out. Iron the rectangles of leather between sheets of paper, turning them over regularly until no more moisture comes out. Be careful not to scorch the leather.

[3] Place the transfer-paper images on the leather so that the top end of each label, which will have the hole, is near one end of the leather. Iron the transfers onto the smooth side of the pieces of leather, following the manufacturer's instructions. Let cool, then peel off the backing paper.

If you have enough leather and you have never attempted iron-on transfers before, do a practice run with the transfer paper before attempting the real thing.

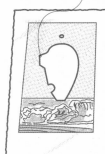

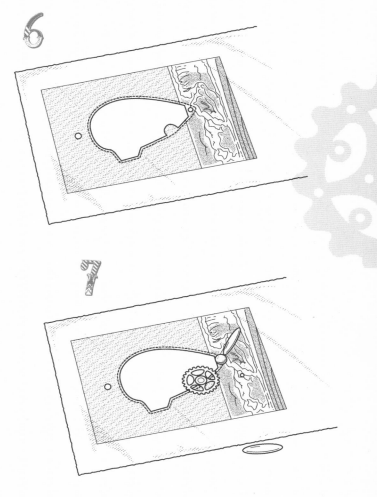

[4] Using sharp scissors, cut out the oval in the frame and the Zeppelin shape from the leather. Using the window template on page 122, cut out two windows from the clear plastic, making them large enough to completely cover the shaped holes. Run a line of solvent-based contact adhesive around the back of each shaped hole and quickly press on the plastic.

[5] With the leather transfer side down, plastic side up, under the foot of a sewing machine, sew ¹⁄₁₆ inch (1.5 mm) from the edge around the oval hole, using dark brown topstitching thread.

[6] Change to beige thread to sew around the Zeppelin shape, making a point at the tail end of the Zeppelin. Pull the thread ends through to the back, knot, and trim. Punch a hole for the plain rivet within the point on the tail of the Zeppelin, avoiding the stitches. Set the rivet.

[7] Punch a hole for the jean rivet within the wheel arch of the Zeppelin. Drill the spoke wheel watch gear hole to fit over the jean rivet, if necessary. Set the rivet through the spoke wheel gear and the leather. Position the cuff link backs on each side of the Zeppelin tail as shown in the photo on page 62 and mark where the loops fall. Punch a hole through each mark.

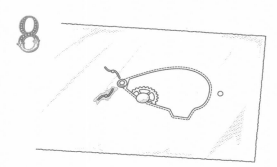

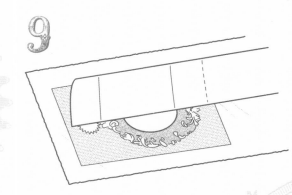

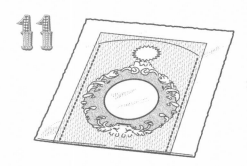

[8] Cut two 1¼-inch (30 mm) lengths of 18 gauge (1 mm) wire. Push the cuff link loops through the holes from the front and push one end of the wire through the loop on the back. Bend the wires into an S shape as shown to secure, and cut shorter, if necessary. Mix up a small amount of two-part epoxy adhesive and use this to cover and seal the wires.

[9] Fold the label outline template in half lengthwise to create a centered line, then open it up and lay it on the oval frame and cog label, aligning the fold line down the center; the solid lines on the template should correspond to points on the image. Draw around the template in ballpoint pen over the printed image, and also mark the dotted fold line at the bottom of the label. Repeat on the Zeppelin label.

[10] Fold the leather under along the marked fold line and tap along the fold line with the hammer to make a sharp crease. Open the fold out again and run a line of latex adhesive on the back of the leather and along the edges of the label. Press together.

[11] Using dark brown topstitching thread for the oval frame and beige thread for the Zeppelin, machine sew up both sides 1/16 inch (1.5 mm) inside the pen line. Use big stitches and sew back and forth at each end of the stitches to secure. Stop sewing ⅛ inch (3 mm) short of the curved edge line on each side. Trim the thread ends.

[12] Trim the side of each label along the pen line with a metal ruler and utility knife. Cut the curve around the top of each label using the utility knife or sharp scissors. Cut a piece of card stock to fit inside the label.

[13] Dilute the gold paint and use it to paint across the frame image, then use full-strength paint to pick out all the highlights on the image. Let dry.

[14] On the oval frame label, punch a hole through the center of the printed cog through both layers, and push the brad fastener through. Thread the ball chain around the brad arms between the layers of leather and join it into a loop with the connector. Open the arms of the brad on the back of the label.

[15] Punch the marked hole in the Zeppelin label through both layers and set an eyelet in each layer of leather. Fold the leather cord in half and thread the loop through the eyelets, then pull the ends through the loop and knot together.

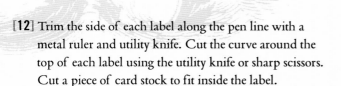

EYEGLASS CASE

The 26 bead caps do not have to be identical—just make sure that you have pairs of each type, because you need two on each U pin holding down the chains.

If you want to conceal the fittings on the inside, make a thin quilted pad in the same way as the fabric mask for the goggles (see page 118) and glue it to the inside of the eyeglass case.

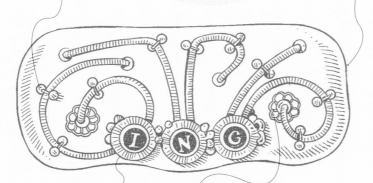

You could omit the eyelets in the holes beneath the bezels, but it's a good place to practice eyelet setting because the bezels will cover them later. Set the eyelets using setting pliers or use an eyelet setting kit with a hammer.

If you need to drill the hole in the filigree connector, you might need an extra connector to practice drilling first.

YOU WILL NEED

- 3 vintage typewriter keys in your chosen initials
- 3 raw brass 23 mm round bezel connectors
- 4 brass thick 9 mm washers
- Dark-colored, leather-look hard eyeglass case
- 18 gauge (1 mm) vintage bronze wire
- 10 gunmetal 3/16 in. (5 mm) eyelets
- 16-in. (40-cm) lengths of 3 different 3 mm chains
- 26 brass 5 mm bead caps
- 2 brass 15 mm round filigree connectors
- 2 brass 1/4 in. (6 mm) eyelets
- Hammer
- Fine (P600) wet and dry sandpaper
- Two-part epoxy adhesive
- Awl
- Wire cutters
- Round-nose pliers
- Craft drill
- 1/16 in. (1.5 mm) metal drill bit
- Heavy-duty 3/16 in. (5 mm) and 1/4 in. (6 mm) punch
- 3/16 in. (5 mm) and 1/4 in. (6 mm) drill bits (optional)
- Small round metal file (optional)
- Eyelet setting tool for 3/16 in. (5 mm) and 1/4 in. (6 mm) eyelets
- Post and vise (optional)
- Superglue gel

CHAINS, EYELETS, AND BEAD CAPS combined with vintage typewriter keys are used to create the ultimate steampunk eyeglass case. A utilitarian accessory becomes a richly decorated artwork full of industrial styling. Make the letters your initials for the ultimate in personal style.

Note: If you cannot find four washers thick enough, make four stacks of thin washers and stick them together with superglue gel— or use four flat beads.

HOW TO MAKE THE EYEGLASS CASE

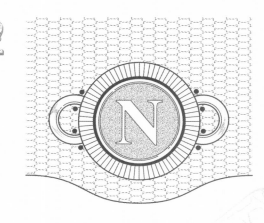

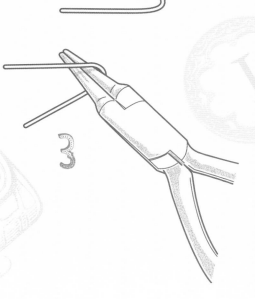

[1] Flatten the backs of the typewriter keys with gentle taps of the hammer and smooth any rough edges with the wet and dry sandpaper. Mix up a small amount of two-part epoxy adhesive and use it to glue each key onto the center of a round bezel connector. Let dry.

[2] Use a brass washer that is thick enough to raise the bezel away from the eyeglass case, so that the chains can pass beneath. Find the center front edge of the case and position one bezel with a washer beneath each of the side loops. Using the awl, mark four holes in the case on each side of the bezel, as shown. Remove the bezel and washers and press harder in each hole with the awl to make a guide hole for the drill.

[3] Cut 12 lengths of 18 gauge (1 mm) wire, 2 inches (50 mm) long, and fold each length over the round-nose pliers to make 12 U-shaped wire pins. Drill the eight holes in the eyeglass case marked in step 2, using a 1/16-inch (1.5-mm) drill bit.

✿ **Note**: Vintage typewriter keys are becoming increasingly harder to find and you may not want to destroy an old typewriter, so try making your own vintage-style typewriter keys. Choose a suitable typewriter-style font—such as Courier—on your computer and print out the required letters at around size 20 pt. or larger on plain, glossy paper. Cut out each letter with a round punch. Darken the white edges of the punched-out letter with black permanent marker. Glue each letter to the center of a suitable sized brass-rimmed button. Apply a coat of clear lacquer to the surface to protect the letter from damage and to help give the "key" an antique look.

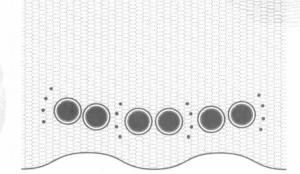

[4] Put the centered bezel back in place, with a washer under each side loop. Add another bezel on each side, so that the adjacent side loops overlap. Push one U pin over the edges of each pair of loops, through the washer beneath, and into the holes in the case. Fold over the arms of the U pins inside the case to hold everything temporarily in place. Position the two outside bezels on the case at a slight angle, place another two washers under the outermost side loops, and mark four holes on each side with the awl, as in step 2.

[5] Remove all the U pins, bezels, and washers. (Discard the four U pins, which are now bent, because it will be easier to guide straight pins into the holes.) Drill the eight new holes marked at the outer edges. Place the washers back in position temporarily and position two eyelets between each pair of washers. Mark the center of each eyelet. Remove the washers and eyelets.

[6] Punch the ³⁄₁₆-inch (5-mm) eyelet holes (or drill the holes, then neaten the edges with a small, round file). Set six of the gunmetal-color eyelets into the case, using the eyelet setting tool. You might need to set up a small post in a vise to act as support inside the case underneath each eyelet as you work, because the inside of the case is not flat.

[7] Cut each of the three lengths of round chain in half and push one end of each length into the eyeleted holes by about 1 inch (25 mm).

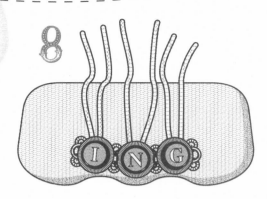

[8] With the chains in position, use the remaining eight U pins to pin on the three bezels with the washers beneath. This time, pass the outer arm of each U pin through a 5 mm bead cap before it goes through the case. If this means that the bezels no longer lie flat, flatten the eight bead caps gently with a hammer first. Fold the U-pin arms down inside the case to secure everything.

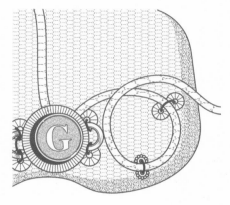

[9] Make nine more wire U pins as in step 3, but using 1⅜-inch (35-mm) lengths of wire, then start positioning one chain at a time. Mark two holes on each side of the chain at intervals, move the chain to one side to make guide holes with the awl, then drill ¹⁄₁₆-inch (1.5-mm) holes. Thread a shorter U pin over the chain, threading a bead cap onto each arm before pushing it into the case. Bend the U-pin arms over on the inside of the case to secure in place. Repeat until all the chains are in position.

[10] When you have pinned the chains down, make a mark where the end of each chain will go back into the case. Take a reference photograph, then remove the chains, U pins, bezels, and washers from the case again. Punch a hole through each filigree connector large enough to hold a ¼-inch (6-mm) brass eyelet. If your punch is not powerful enough for this, you will have to drill the hole carefully instead.

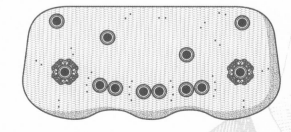

[11] Punch a hole for an eyelet at each mark where the chain end needs to go back into the case. Set in the six eyelets, putting a filigree connector behind each of the two brass eyelets. This step is complex, so be patient and careful and take your time.

[12] Now begin the final assembly—it is a good idea to make eight new, long U pins and nine shorter U pins, as in steps 3 and 9, because the original ones will now have bent arms. Secure all the chains on first as before, this time pushing the final end of each chain through the appropriate eyelet.

[13] On the inside, leave all the chain ends long for the moment. Bend the U-pin arms toward each other on the inside, so that they are tight and flat against the inside of the case. Glue around each chain where it goes through an eyelet. If there are any big gaps left in the eyelet holes, carefully fill with superglue gel from the inside.

[14] If any section of chain on the outside of the case is loose, use a little superglue gel to hold it in place. Pin on the bezels, washers, and bead caps, again bending the U-pin arms flat on the inside. Cut the chain ends nearly flush to the inside of the case and trim the wire arms shorter if they do not lie flat because of the curve of the inside edge of the case.

[15] Prop the case up, so that it will stay in place, with the top half facing downward. Cover all the U-pin arms and chain eyelets with a layer of two-part epoxy adhesive to seal and secure them in place. Let dry.

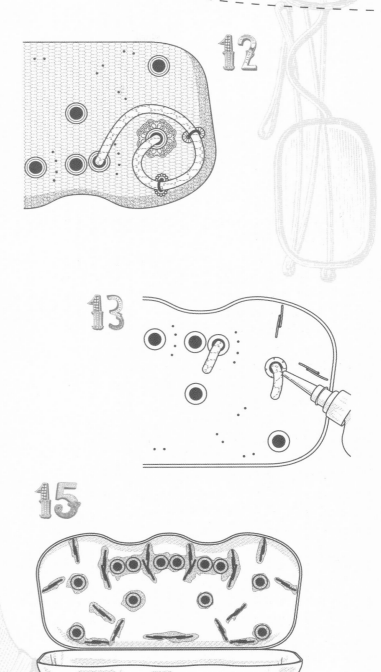

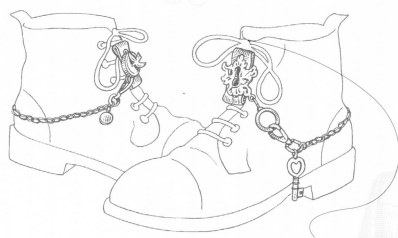

If your boots have hooks at the top for lacing, thread both laces through the top tube of the ornament in opposite directions.

- ❋ 8-in. (20-cm) length of brown leather belting, 1–1¼ in. (25–30 mm) wide and no thicker than ¹⁄₁₆ in. (1.5 mm)
- ❋ Brass 4 mm eyelet
- ❋ Black heavy-duty prewaxed thread
- ❋ 1¼ in. (30 mm) antique copper flying bird pendant
- ❋ Brass medal, about 1 in. (25 mm) diameter
- ❋ 26-in. (65-cm) length of antique gold heavy curb chain
- ❋ 5 antique gold 8 mm jump rings
- ❋ 2 antique gold 1½ in. (40 mm) bag charm clips
- ❋ Small bead pendant
- ❋ Decorative brass key plate, about 1½ x 2 in. (40 x 50 mm)
- ❋ Bronze topstitching thread
- ❋ 4 links of antique brass large etched oval cable chain
- ❋ 23 mm filigree ring
- ❋ Antique gold head pin
- ❋ Raw brass key, about 1¾ in. (45 mm) long
- ❋ Paper and scissors for template
- ❋ Metal ruler
- ❋ Utility knife
- ❋ Black ballpoint pen
- ❋ Leather punch
- ❋ Eyelet setting tool for ³⁄₁₆ in. (5 mm) eyelet
- ❋ Heavy-duty hand sewing needle
- ❋ Craft drill
- ❋ ¹⁄₁₆ in. (1.5 mm) metal drill bit
- ❋ Wire cutters
- ❋ Awl
- ❋ Round-nose pliers
- ❋ Flat-nose pliers

L ACE-UP BOOTS are an essential part of the look of times past, but add these extra ornamentations for a deceptively elaborate effect. In fact, they are really easy to make, with only simple sewing skills. You can make both boots the same if you prefer, or adapt the design to embellish shoes instead.

❋ **Note**: See page 123 for the boot ornaments template. If you can't find a suitable bead pendant for the ornaments, make one by threading a round bead and a bead cap onto a head pin. Cut the pin down and use round-nose pliers to curl the wire end into a loop.

❁ HOW TO MAKE THE BOOT LIVERIES

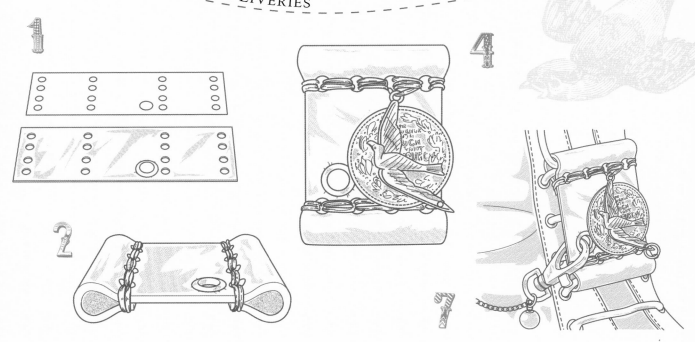

[1] Scan or trace the template on page 123 and cut out. Draw around it on a section of belt and trim the leather to length using the metal ruler and utility knife. Mark the holes on the leather with the ballpoint pen, then punch out the holes. Set in the 3/16-inch (5-mm) eyelet.

[2] Roll the cut ends of the strap ornament over, aligning the rows of holes. Using a doubled length of prewaxed thread, sew through the holes to make two tubes for the laces.

[3] If the flying bird pendant does not have a second hole near the bottom, drill one toward the end of the bottom wing.

[4] Using another doubled length of prewaxed thread, sew the bird and the medal onto the strap through their hanging loops and a stitch hole in the leather right of center. Knot the threads on the back.

[5] Lace up the right boot to just above the ankle so that the laces are horizontal. Thread one lace through the bottom tube of the strap ornament, continue to lace up the boots to the top of the ornament, and then thread one lace through the top tube, where it lines up with nearest eyelet in the boot. Finish lacing and tie.

[6] Cut the curb chain in half and attach one end to the hole in the bottom of the bird's wing, using an 8 mm jump ring. Attach a bag charm clip through the eyelet in the strap ornament and measure how long the chain needs to be to go right around the back of the boot, then attach the chain to the end of the bag charm clip.

[7] Cut the chain to length, then add the last link and the bead pendant to another 8 mm jump ring, threading this through the ring at the bottom of the bag charm clip.

[8] Make a second leather strap ornament, as in steps 1 and 2, but without the eyelet. Lay the key plate on the middle of the strap and work out several stitch holes and holes for the chains. Drill any additional holes required in the key plate, then lay it over the strap ornament and mark the stitch holes on the leather with the awl.

[9] Remove the key plate and make the holes through the leather with the awl or small punch. Sew the key plate onto the strap ornament, using doubled topstitching thread, oversewing several times and knotting at the back. Lace the ornament onto the boot as described in step 5.

[10] Remove one of the oval links from the short length of chain and attach it through a hole in the key plate. Attach the remaining length of curb chain to it, using an 8 mm jump ring.

[11] Take the filigree ring and open it up a little with pliers to push the head of the head pin inside, then close it again to hold the head pin in place. Wrap the wire of the head pin around an end link in the remaining links of oval chain, back around itself, and then cut off.

[12] Open the other end link of the oval chain to attach it to an outside hole in the key plate. Attach the bag charm clip to the filigree ring, work out how long the chain needs to be to go around the back of the boot and reach the end of the bag charm clip, and cut the chain to length.

[13] Attach the end of the chain to the bag charm clip, using an 8 mm jump ring. Add the key to the bag charm clip, using an 8 mm jump ring.

POCKET GAUNTLETS

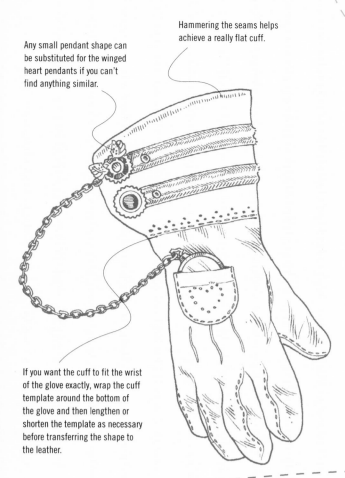

Any small pendant shape can be substituted for the winged heart pendants if you can't find anything similar.

Hammering the seams helps achieve a really flat cuff.

If you want the cuff to fit the wrist of the glove exactly, wrap the cuff template around the bottom of the glove and then lengthen or shorten the template as necessary before transferring the shape to the leather.

YOU WILL NEED

- 4 brass 5 mm bead caps
- 4 raw brass spoke wheel watch gears, about 1 in. (25 mm) diameter
- 4 antique brass head pins
- 2 antique brass coin pendants, about ⅝ in. (15 mm) diameter
- 2 winged heart pendants, about 1½ x 1 in. (35 x 25 mm)
- 4 amber 2 mm rhinestones
- 40 in. (1 m) length of ⅝ in. (15 mm) grosgrain ribbon
- 80 in. (2 m) length of ³⁄₁₆ in. (5 mm) braid trimming
- Piece of ¹⁄₃₂ in. (1 mm) mid-brown leather, 16 x 24 in. (40 x 60 cm)
- Masking tape
- Dark brown topstitching thread
- Pair of well-worn, dark brown leather gloves
- 8 antique brass 8 mm plain rivets
- 24-in. (60-cm) length of brown leather cord
- 4 antique brass 25 mm toggle bars
- 12-in. (30-cm) length of antique brass, large, etched oval cable chain

- Monocle with loop
- Paper and scissors for template
- Small hammer
- Superglue gel
- Small carton or box for working on
- Awl
- Wire cutters
- Small flat metal file
- Sharp scissors
- Fabric/craft adhesive
- Two-part epoxy adhesive for metal
- Round-nose pliers
- Ballpoint pen
- Leather punch
- Latex-based contact adhesive
- Sewing machine with leather needle and heavy needle options
- Card stock to protect surface
- Solvent-based contact adhesive
- Dark brown leather dye (optional)
- Neutral traditional leather shoe dressing (optional)
- Soft cloth (optional)
- Fine (P600) wet and dry sandpaper
- Rivet setting tool

W HO NEEDS PLAIN AND BORING GLOVES when you can wear decorative and useful gauntlets with braided, riveted, and punched cuffs? Note the handy pocket to carry your monocle—which may, of course, be needed at any time to peruse a map or decipher a code.

> ✿ **Note**: See page 126 for the gauntlet templates. The coin used on the gauntlets is a British predecimal three-penny bit pendant, but any suitable brass-colored coin of a similar size to fit on the spoke wheel gear can be substituted.

HOW TO MAKE THE POCKET GAUNTLETS

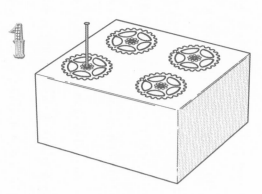

[1] Gently flatten the bead caps with the hammer. Glue each bead cap into the center of a spoke wheel watch gear with dabs of superglue gel. Punch four holes in the top of the box with the awl. Place each spoke wheel watch gear over a hole and drop a head pin through the center hole and into the hole in the box. Let dry.

[2] Snip the loop off each coin pendant and file smooth. Glue the coins to the front of two of the spoke wheel gears and glue the winged hearts to the other two gears, using dabs of superglue. Add one of the rhinestones to each coin and to each heart.

[3] Cut the ribbon into four equal lengths and the braid trimming into eight equal lengths. Glue one length of braid down each edge of the lengths of ribbon, using fabric/craft adhesive. Press down firmly and let dry.

[4] Make sure the coins and winged hearts are securely attached to the spoke wheel gears by spreading two-part epoxy adhesive over the back of the gears, where it will not show on the front. Trim each head pin to $\frac{1}{16}$ inch (1.5 mm) and use round-nose pliers to curl the wire end into a loop.

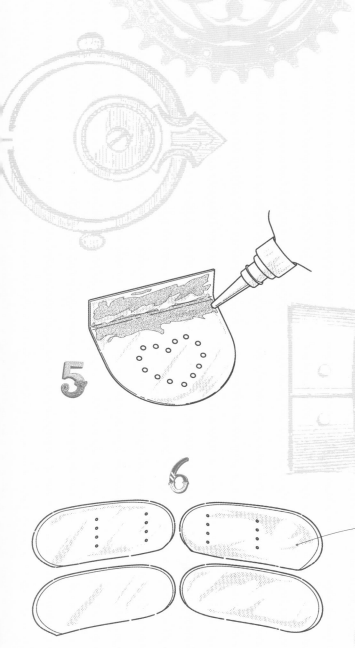

[5] Scan or trace the monocle pocket template on page 126 and cut out. Draw around it on the back of the leather with a ballpoint pen. Cut out the monocle pocket and punch the holes to make the heart design. Spread a thin layer of latex-base contact adhesive on the back in a narrow strip, from the straight edge to the dotted line marked on the template, and let dry. Fold the straight edge to the dotted line and press down to secure.

[6] Scan or trace the cuff template on page 126 and cut out. Draw around it on the back of the leather with a ballpoint pen and cut out. Mark the dots for the cuff link holes and the ribbon braid holes, but not the decorative punched detail along one edge at this stage. Repeat with the template turned over to make a second cuff the mirror image of the first. Cut out the cuffs, leaving a ³⁄₁₆-inch (5-mm) seam allowance around the outer edge lines but cutting directly along the line below the dotted detail. Punch two sets of four holes in each cuff for the ribbon braid. Cut another two cuffs, first with the template the right side up and then reversed, but do not mark or punch any holes on these pieces.

[7] Place a pair of punched and unmarked cuffs right sides together. It is hard to pin leather accurately and pins would leave holes, so instead use short strips of masking tape around the outside edge to stick the layers together.

If you can find leather to match the gloves or if you want the cuffs to contrast with the gloves, you can omit the breaking down and dyeing stage in step 11.

[**8**] Using topstitching thread, machine sew around the outer edge lines, leaving the edge that will have the punched detail open. Sew back and forth at each end of the stitches to secure. Remove the masking tape and cut the top layer seam allowance down to ¹⁄₁₆ inch (1.5 mm). Repeat steps 7 and 8 for the other cuff.

[**9**] Turn both cuffs right side out. Push the stitches from inside to get the seam as flat as possible. Work the stitches right to the edge, then tap the edge with a hammer to fold and flatten it, working on a flat, hard surface protected with a layer of card stock. Hammer both sides of the cuffs.

[**10**] Fold each cuff in half and stretch until the two layers lie flat. Run a strip of solvent-based contact adhesive about ½ inch (10 mm) wide along the inside of the open edges. Let dry and secure together. Fold the cuffs in half again and stretch until the layers lie flat.

[**11**] Lay the paper template on top of the cuff and mark the punched edge detail with the ballpoint pen. Punch out the decorative pattern on each cuff through both layers of leather. Break down the leather (see page 15) and dye it to blend in with your gloves, if necessary. You can only make the leather darker—if your gloves are a light color, then dye them darker to match the cuffs. If the gloves have a shiny finish, treat the cuffs with a traditional dressing and buff them with a soft cloth to match.

[**12**] Cut the stitches of the seam on the outside of each glove to a position level with the start of the little finger. This will make it easier later to sew on the monocle pocket and the cuff.

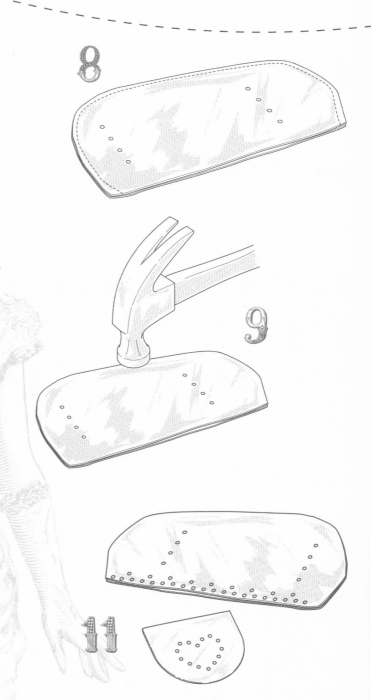

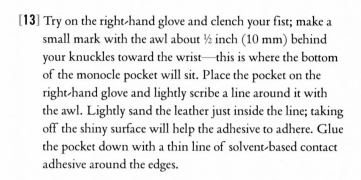

[13] Try on the right-hand glove and clench your fist; make a small mark with the awl about ½ inch (10 mm) behind your knuckles toward the wrist—this is where the bottom of the monocle pocket will sit. Place the pocket on the right-hand glove and lightly scribe a line around it with the awl. Lightly sand the leather just inside the line; taking off the shiny surface will help the adhesive to adhere. Glue the pocket down with a thin line of solvent-based contact adhesive around the edges.

[14] Machine sew the pocket onto the glove using a fairly large stitch, sewing back and forth at each end of the stitches to secure. Pull the threads to the inside and knot off.

[15] Try on the glove again and mark the cuff position—the seam at the glove should sit level with the wrist bone. Scribe a line all the way around the bottom edge of both gloves in line with the mark. Sand off the surface of the bottom edge of the glove below the line, and run a thin line of solvent-based contact adhesive around the edge. Run another thin line of adhesive on the side of the cuff without ribbon braid holes, between the punched detail and the top edge. Let dry, then secure the cuff to the glove. Repeat on the other glove.

[16] Machine sew the cuffs in place, sewing just below the dotted detail. Sew back and forth at each end of the stitches to secure, pulling the threads to the back and knotting off. It doesn't matter if the cuff doesn't quite reach the end of glove or is too long—just make sure it is positioned equally on the top and palm sides of the glove and the ribbon and braid holes are on the outside.

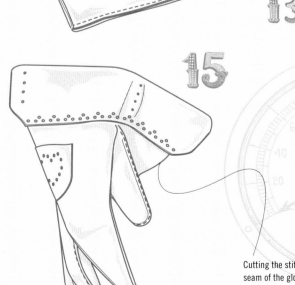

Cutting the stitches on the side seam of the glove means you can partly flatten the glove to make it easier to sew on the monocle pocket and the cuff.

❋ HOW TO MAKE THE POCKET GAUNTLETS

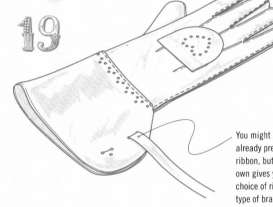

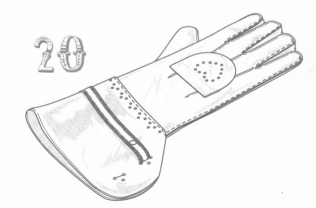

[17] Trim the excess from the bottom edge of each glove, as close to the stitch line as possible. Glue the cut seam of each glove back together with latex adhesive, then sew it closed again.

[18] Align the cuff edges and punch two small holes through all layers at the marks for the cuff links on each cuff. Using scissors, cut four neat slits in each cuff, cutting through one layer of the cuff only, between the pairs of punched holes made for the ribbon braid.

[19] Trim the ends of the ribbon braid. Starting at the uppermost slit nearest the cuff link holes, turn the ribbon braid upside down and slide 1 inch (25 mm) between the two layers of leather. Fold the ribbon braid back and around the glove, then slide the other end into the corresponding slit on the palm side of the glove.

[20] Make sure the ribbon braid is in the correct position, then punch a hole through all the layers of leather and ribbon braid ¾ inch (20 mm) from the slit. Set a rivet in the hole. Repeat steps 19 and 20 for the other strip of ribbon braid and on the other glove.

You might be able to find already prepared braided ribbon, but making up your own gives you a little more choice of ribbon color and type of braid trimming.

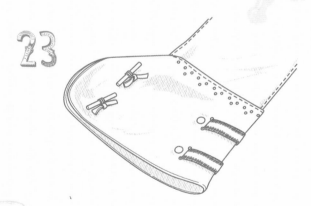

[21] Remove the end of each length of ribbon braid from the slits on the palm side of the glove and trim to extend 1 inch (25 mm) beyond the slits in the leather. Slide the ribbon braid back into the slits and hold so that it lies flat around the cuff. Punch a hole through all layers ¼ inch (6 mm) from the slit and set in a rivet. Make sure the second line of ribbon braid is parallel to the first before riveting.

[22] Cut the leather cord into four equal lengths. Thread one length through the loop on the back of one of the coin cuff links made earlier, then bring the cord ends through the cuff link hole nearest the glove, pushing them through both layers of the cuff.

[23] Thread a toggle bar onto one end of the cord on the other side of the glove, tie the ends in a knot close to the cuff, and trim the excess. Repeat for the winged heart cuff link in the other cuff link hole. Add the cuff links to the other glove in the same way.

[24] Open a link at each end of the cable chain. Fasten one end to the monocle loop and the other to a hole in the spoke wheel gear of the winged cuff link on the right-hand glove.

LEATHER PHONE CASE

THIS CASE IS DESIGNED to fit most midsized cell phones, but lay your own phone over the template before you start; you can add a little more width or length to the template if it doesn't fit. The choice of photograph for the center of the compass and trimming for the chain is entirely up to you—customize these elements with as much or as little steampunk detail and hardware as you desire.

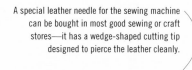

A special leather needle for the sewing machine can be bought in most good sewing or craft stores—it has a wedge-shaped cutting tip designed to pierce the leather cleanly.

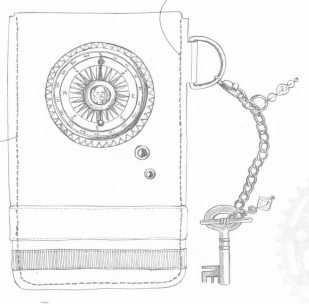

Be as accurate as possible when sewing leather, because the holes the needle makes are permanent and will remain, even if any incorrect stitches are later removed.

⚙ **Note**: See pages 120–121 for the cell phone case templates. The exact beads used for the ornamented chain are listed, but substitute your own selection, if you prefer.

⚙ YOU WILL NEED

- Piece of iron-on transfer paper (for light-colored fabric), 6¼ in. (16 cm) square
- Piece of heavy white cotton fabric, 2¾ in. (7 cm) square
- Piece of beige leather, 6 x 4 in. (15 x 10 cm)
- Mixed metallic ⅛ in. (3 mm) eyelets
- Piece of dark brown leather, 8 x 8¾ in. (20 x 22 cm)
- Antique brass 13 mm flower bead cap
- Mixed metallic ³⁄₁₆ in. (5 mm) eyelets
- Brown topstitching thread
- Black and olive-green heavy-duty sewing thread
- 1½-in. (40-mm) length of ¾ in. (20 mm) black hook-and-loop tape

- Plain brass key plate, about 1 in. (25 mm) diameter
- 2 brass-colored mini craft brads
- Metallic ⁵⁄₁₆ in. (8 mm) eyelet
- Personal picture or photograph to fit the ⁵⁄₁₆ in. (8 mm) eyelet
- 4-in. (10-cm) length of ⅝ in. (15 mm) olive-green velvet ribbon
- 4-in. (10-cm) length of ½ in. (10 mm) olive-green grosgrain ribbon
- Antique gold D-ring, 1 in. (25 mm) wide
- Small scrap of thin, flat leather
- Small brass bead
- Small brass washer
- Antique gold 20 mm heavy sprung hook

- 3-in. (7.5-cm) length of antique gold medium chain
- Antique gold 25 mm toggle bar
- 2 antique gold 25 mm head pins
- Light green 4 mm diamond-shaped glass bead
- Clear 4 mm diamond-shaped glass bead
- 2 antique gold 8 mm jump rings
- Small metal key
- Light green rocaille bead
- Lilac 8 mm Swarovski bead
- Cloudy green 3 mm faceted glass bead
- Paper and scissors for template
- Leather punch
- Iron
- Ballpoint pen

- Awl
- Eyelet setting tool for ⅛ in. (3 mm), ³⁄₁₆ in. (5 mm), and ⁵⁄₁₆ in. (8 mm) eyelets
- Hammer
- Solvent-based contact adhesive
- Sewing machine with leather needle and heavy needle options
- Fine black permanent marker pen
- Ruler
- Fine (P600) wet and dry sandpaper (optional)
- Latex-based contact adhesive
- Flat-nose pliers
- Round-nose pliers
- Wire cutters

HOW TO MAKE THE LEATHER PHONE CASE

TEMPLATES

[1] Scan or trace all the leather phone case templates on pages 120–121 and cut out. Use the punch to punch out all the eyelet holes as indicated on the templates.

[2] Scan the compass image and the background image and print both out on a piece of iron-on transfer paper. If you don't have a scanner, this job can be done at a photocopying or printing store.

[3] Cut out the compass image and the background image from the transfer paper, leaving a ¼-inch (5-mm) border outside the image all around the edges.

[4] Iron the compass transfer, image-side down, onto the white cotton fabric, following the manufacturer's instructions. Let cool, then peel off the backing paper and set aside.

[5] Set the iron on as high a heat as possible, without steam, and press the piece of beige leather on the wrong (rough) side for about a minute and a half. It will shrink slightly.

[6] Iron the background transfer, image-side down, onto the right (smooth) side of the beige leather as before. Let cool, then peel off the backing paper.

BACK

[7] Lay the template for the back of the cell phone case on the right side of the beige leather and draw around it lightly with a ballpoint pen. Use an awl to indent small points at the edges where the leather strip will be added, at the corners for the placement for the hook-and-loop tape strip, and to mark the eyelet positions. Cut out the leather back, leaving an ⅛-inch (3-mm) seam allowance around the whole piece.

[8] Use the leather punch to make two ⅛-inch (3-mm) holes in the beige leather at the marked positions for the eyelets. Use the eyelet setter to add an ⅛-inch (3-mm) eyelet to each hole.

[9] Cut a strip 4 inches (10 cm) long and ¾ inch (20 mm) wide from the dark brown leather. Use gentle taps of the hammer to flatten the flower bead cap. Punch a ⅛-inch (3-mm) hole in the center of the flower bead cap and a matching hole centered on the width of the leather strip and 1¼ inches (30 mm) from one end. Use a ⅛-inch (3-mm) eyelet and the eyelet setter to attach the flower to the leather strip. Add a ³⁄₁₆-inch (5-mm) and a ⅛-inch (3-mm) eyelet to one side of the flower in the same way.

[10] Glue the leather strip in place across the back piece in the marked position, using a small amount of solvent-based contact adhesive. Then, using brown topstitching thread, machine sew all around the strip close to the edges. Trim the ends of the strip flush with the edges of the back piece.

[11] Rethread the sewing machine with black thread and sew the hook side of the hook-and-loop tape in the marked position on the front of the back piece, using a zigzag stitch.

FRONT

[12] Place the front and the flap lining templates on the dark brown leather and draw around the outlines, using a ballpoint pen. Use an awl to indent small points on the front piece to show the edge of the flap, top of the case, eyelet, compass positions, and the ribbon placement. Mark the position of the hook-and-loop tape on the flap lining piece in the same way. Mark a ⅛-inch (3-mm) seam allowance around the flap lining piece, and around the outer edge of the front piece, from the mark for the top of the case on the left side around the bottom to the mark for the top of the case on the right side, but not around the strip of leather on the right side that will hold the D-ring.

[13] Cut out the front piece, including the hole for the key plate. Cut out the flap lining.

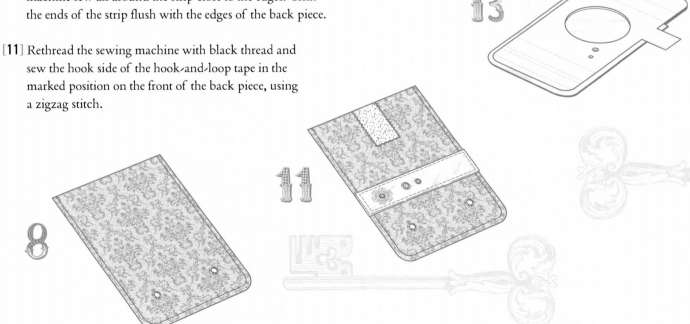

HOW TO MAKE THE LEATHER PHONE CASE

[**14**] Using black thread and a zigzag stitch, machine sew the loop piece of the hook-and-loop tape in place on the right (smooth) side of the flap lining. Turn the flap lining over and use a black marker pen to color in the area on the wrong (rough) side that will show through the key hole in the key plate.

[**15**] Spread a thin layer of solvent-based contact adhesive on the wrong side of the flap lining and on the corresponding wrong side of the flap section of the front. Wait for a minute or two, then press the lining and front together to adhere, lining up the scalloped edges as neatly as possible.

[**16**] Lay the paper template labeled "stitch detail" on top of the right side of the front flap, so that the curved top edge sits just inside the middle scallop. Draw around the curved side of the stitch detail with a ballpoint pen, add two horizontal lines on either side, using a ruler, then continue the lines up and around the side scallops just inside the edge, as shown in the illustration. Using brown topstitching thread, machine sew along the ballpoint lines.

[**17**] Position the key plate over the hole cut for it in the front piece and mark the fitting holes on either side of the plate with the awl. Turn the front piece over and push the key plate under the flap lining and into position. Turn back over again and push the awl through the marked holes, through both layers of leather, and the holes on each side of the key plate. Push a brass-colored mini brad through each hole and open up on the back of the flap to hold the key plate in place.

[**18**] Cut out the fabric compass and set the ⁵⁄₁₆-inch (8-mm) eyelet in the center. If you prefer, you can distress the eyelet a little with wet and dry sandpaper to give it an aged look.

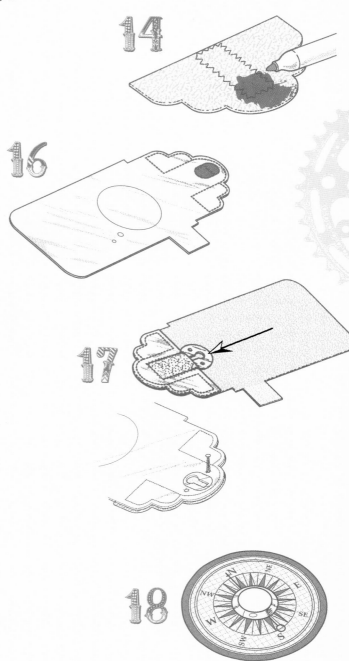

[19] Use the eyelet hole in the compass to select a suitable area of the image you have chosen for the middle of the compass. Cut out the image so that it is larger than the eyelet hole but smaller than the compass, then machine sew it in position on the front piece of the case, using a circle of small zigzag stitches.

[20] Use a few tiny dabs of solvent-based contact adhesive to tack the compass in place on the front piece, centering it over the photograph. Using brown topstitching thread, machine sew a neat circle of small zigzag stitches to secure the compass more firmly.

[21] Punch the appropriate holes and set a ³⁄₁₆-inch (5-mm) and a ⅛-inch (3-mm) eyelet below right of the compass, as indicated on the template.

[22] Use a few tiny dabs of latex-based contact adhesive to tack the strips of velvet and grosgrain ribbon across the front piece in the marked positions. Using olive-green thread, machine sew the ribbons in place, sewing close to the edges along each length.

[23] Trim the ribbon ends so that they extend only ½ inch (10 mm) beyond the sides of the front piece. Add a little latex adhesive on the wrong side of the ribbon ends and on the wrong side of the front case, wait for a moment, then fold the ribbons neatly over the leather edge and secure down on the back.

[24] With the front piece wrong-side up, thread the D-ring onto the side strap. Spread a thin layer of solvent-based contact adhesive on the last ¼ inch (6 mm) of the back of the strap and on the back of the case where it is to be secured down. Wait for a moment or two, then press the surfaces together to adhere.

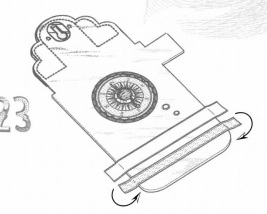

JOINING BACK AND FRONT

[25] Cut three small oval or round pieces from the scrap of thin leather and punch holes to match the eyelet holes. Using latex adhesive, secure one over the back of each eyelet on the wrong side of both the front and back pieces, as shown, so that the eyelets cannot scratch your cell phone.

[26] Spread a thin line of solvent-based contact adhesive along the ⅛-inch (3-mm) seam allowance, on the wrong sides of both the back and front pieces of the case. Wait for a moment or two, then align the back and front and press together to adhere.

[27] Using a leather needle and brown topstitching thread, machine sew around the three sides of the case, following the ballpoint line. Go back and forth twice at each end of the seam to strengthen the tops of the case sides.

[28] Thread a small round brass bead and a washer onto the heavy sprung hook. Thread the chain onto the hook, then clip the hook onto the D-ring and swing it around so that the D-ring sits in the ring at the end of the hook. Use pliers to open and close the end ring on the antique gold toggle bar to fasten it onto the free end of the chain.

[29] Take one of the gold head pins and thread on the two diamond-shaped glass beads. Cut off the excess wire and use round-nose pliers to curl the wire end into a loop. Thread the loop onto a jump ring. Open the jump ring, thread it through the ring at the head of the key, then close it. Thread the toggle bar through the head of the key.

[30] Thread the other head pin with a light green rocaille bead, a lilac faceted Swarovski bead, and a cloudy green faceted bead. Curl the wire end into a loop as before and fasten it a few links down from the top of the chain, using the remaining jump ring.

VINTAGE · BILLFOLD

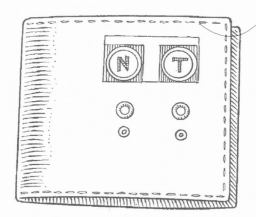

When topstitching, always
work with the right side of
the piece uppermost in the
sewing machine.

✿ YOU WILL NEED

- ✿ 3 sheets of 8½ x 11 in./A4 iron-on transfer paper (for light-colored fabric)
- ✿ Piece of very thin, crisp white linen, 12 x 26 in. (30 x 65 cm)
- ✿ Piece of 1/16 in. (1.5 mm) olive-green leather, 4¾ x 9 in. (12 x 23 cm)
- ✿ Brown topstitching thread
- ✿ 2 antique brass 3/16 in. (5 mm) eyelets
- ✿ 2 antique brass 1/8 in. (3 mm) eyelets
- ✿ Brown sewing thread
- ✿ Iron
- ✿ Paper and scissors for template
- ✿ Leather punch
- ✿ Black ballpoint pen
- ✿ Metal ruler
- ✿ Craft knife and extra blades
- ✿ Sewing machine with standard needle, leather needle, and heavy needle options
- ✿ Sharp scissors
- ✿ Eyelet setting tool for 3/16 in. (5 mm) and 1/8 in. (3 mm) eyelets
- ✿ Pencil
- ✿ Solvent-based contact adhesive
- ✿ Adhesive spatula

✿ Note: See See pages 124–125 for the billfold templates. First practice spreading the adhesive thinly onto the back of a scrap of leather, if possible. The layer of adhesive on the billfold leather needs to be thin so that the sewing machine needle does not become sticky when sewing through the leather later.

F ORGET THAT MODERN WALLET and use one evocative of days gone by. You may not be able to flash genuine Victorian money, but this vintage-look billfold will make modern banknotes look quite the thing. The ideal accessory for a night out, it brings a true sense of occasion to even the simplest purchase.

✿ HOW TO MAKE THE VINTAGE BILLFOLD

BILLFOLD EXTERIOR

[1] Scan the image of the typewriter keys on page 124 and print out on a sheet of iron-on transfer paper. Cut around the two initials you need, leaving at least another key width all around. Iron the transfer onto the linen, following the manufacturer's instructions. Let cool, then peel off the backing paper.

[2] Trim around the two letters you need, cutting down the center of the neighboring keys on each side. Fold back the side edges to make a strip a fraction wider than the width of the typewriter key circle.

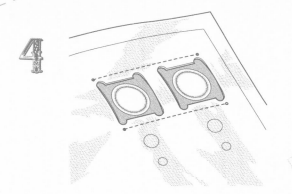

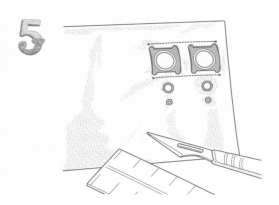

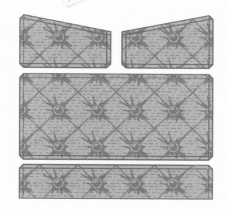

[3] Cut a rectangle of paper 3½ x 8½ inches (9 x 21 cm). In the top right-hand corner, punch the holes as shown on the top right-hand corner template on page 124. Draw around the edge of the paper on the right side of the leather, using the ballpoint pen. Mark all the holes with the pen.

[4] Punch out the two groups of four tiny holes with the leather punch. Cut slits between four pairs of holes, as indicated on the template, using the metal ruler and a craft knife with a new blade. Thread the top and bottom edges of a letter strip into each pair of slits, centering the letter. Using a leather needle and brown topstitching thread, machine sew above and below each letter near the slits to hold the initials in position. Pull the thread ends through to the back and knot. Trim away any excess from the letter strips with sharp scissors.

[5] Punch out the remaining four holes for the eyelets, then set a large and small eyelet beneath each initial. Cut out the rectangle of leather along the ballpoint line, using the metal ruler and a sharp craft knife.

BILLFOLD INTERIOR

[6] Scan the quilted leather images on pages 124–125 and print out on a piece of iron-on transfer paper. Iron the transfers onto the linen, as before. Cut out the four billfold interior pieces around the edges of the photographic image.

[7] On the reverse, draw a line lightly in pencil ½ inch (10 mm) in from all the edges, except the bottom edge of the piece labeled "top edge." The area between the edge and the pencil line is where the adhesive should be spread.

[8] Spread a thin layer of solvent-based contact adhesive on the back of the four corners of the "behind pockets" piece, the bottom two corners of each "pocket" piece, and the top two corners of the "top edge" piece. Dab the adhesive on and use a spatula to spread it quickly before it starts to set. Let dry. Fold over each corner diagonally in turn, to secure.

[9] Spread a really thin layer of adhesive on the back of the "top edge" piece around the top and side edges, inside the pencil line. Let dry. Fold the three edges over along the black lines and glue down, pressing firmly to make crisp folds. Spread adhesive, fold, and secure the four sides of the "behind pockets" piece in the same way, then the sloped and bottom edges only of the two "pocket" pieces.

[10] Using brown sewing thread and a standard needle, machine sew a line ¹⁄₁₆ inch (1.5 mm) in from the sloping edges only on the two "pocket" pieces and the top edge only on the "behind pockets" piece.

[11] Glue down the shorter sides of the two "pocket" pieces as in step 9. Fold over the longer sides to crease them, but open the folds out again before the next step.

[12] Run a very thin line of solvent-based contact adhesive just in from the edge on the back of one "pocket" piece only, along the short side and the bottom edge. Quickly place the pocket in position on the front of the "behind pockets" rectangle, aligning points A and C. Repeat for the other pocket. Let dry thoroughly. Sew down the short side and across the bottom edge, sewing back and forth at each end of the stitches to secure.

[13] Turn the billfold interior over. Fold the long edge of each pocket over the side edges of the "behind pockets" piece. Spread adhesive up to the fold line on each pocket tab and on corresponding strips along the side edges on the back of the "behind pockets" piece. Glue the tabs of the pockets down onto the back of the "behind pockets" piece.

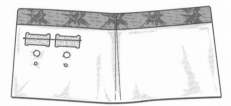

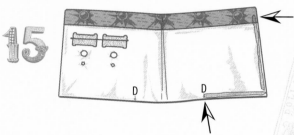

Leave the section between the two Ds unsewn—this allows for the billfold to flex properly when it is opened and closed.

ASSEMBLING THE BILLFOLD

[14] Spread a thin layer of adhesive on the back of the "top edge" piece. On the back of the leather rectangle, spread another thin layer of adhesive in a strip 1 inch (25 mm) wide along the top edge. Let dry. Glue the two pieces together back to back, so that the folded edge of the "top edge" piece aligns with the top edge of the leather rectangle.

[15] Place the completed billfold interior on the back of the leather rectangle to establish where the top of the billfold interior will fall; mark this with a dot on each side edge of the leather, using the ballpoint pen. Mark the two point Ds on the bottom edge of the leather in the same way. Run a very thin line of adhesive around the edge of the leather between the dots on the side and bottom (as indicated by the two arrows on the illustration), and between the same two points on the other side. Add another line of adhesive between the matching points on each side on the back of the billfold interior piece. Let dry.

[16] Glue the billfold interior to the back of the leather rectangle. Turn the billfold over and mark the two point Ds lightly on the right side of the leather. Using a leather needle and brown topstitching thread, machine sew a line around the billfold 1/16 inch (1.5 mm) in from the edge, working from one D right around to the other.

FEATHER FASCINATOR

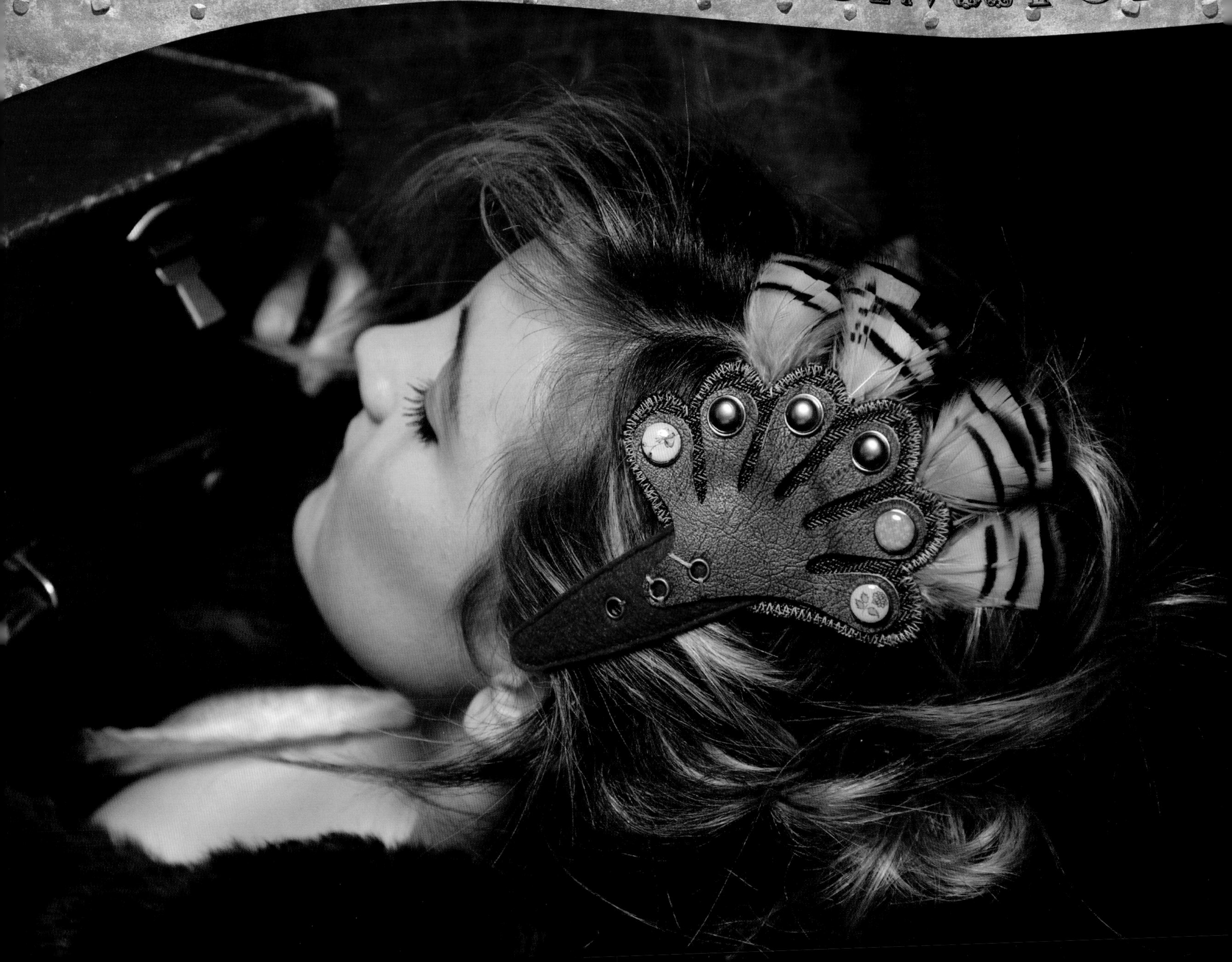

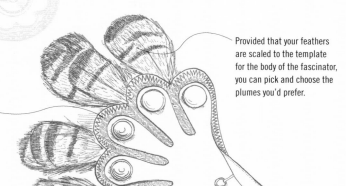

A textured or pebbled leather will give a more artisanal end result. Craft stores often stock small scraps of interesting leathers.

Provided that your feathers are scaled to the template for the body of the fascinator, you can pick and choose the plumes you'd prefer.

Customize your studs further by placing tiny mementos under them—you can buy snap-together glass bezels that are perfect for the job.

YOU WILL NEED

- Piece of dark red/burgundy felt, 12 x 2½ in. (30 x 6.5 cm)
- Dark red/burgundy and beige sewing thread
- 4-in. (10-cm) snap hair clip
- Piece of 1/16 in. (1.5 mm) brown leather, 5 in. (12.5 cm) square
- 3 antique copper 3/16 in. (5 mm) eyelets
- 4-in. (10-cm) square cut from the flat side of a plastic milk or juice carton (see page 115)
- 4-in. (10-cm) length of French partridge feather trim or similar
- Piece of black-and-brown herringbone suiting fabric, 5 in. (12.5 cm) square
- 3 green pearlized 10 mm epoxy brads
- 3 red/green patterned 10 mm epoxy brads
- Green embroidery floss
- Paper and scissors for templates
- Sharp scissors
- Air-erasable marking pen
- Sewing machine with leather needle and heavy needle options
- Awl
- Fine white marking pen
- Hand sewing needle
- Black ballpoint pen
- Leather punch
- Eyelet setting tool for 3/16 in. (5 mm) eyelets
- Fine black permanent marker pen
- 2-in. (50-mm) wide double-sided tape
- Solvent-based contact adhesive
- Adhesive spatula

A FASCINATOR is a bit more than a hair clip, but stops short of being a hat—the perfect ornament for a special steampunk occasion, whether it's the launch of a new Zeppelin or a trip on a steam train. You can customize it further by putting personal images or symbols under the little glass studs. Craft stores offer a wide range of feathers and plumes, so you can choose from a variety of options in terms of size and color.

❋ HOW TO MAKE THE FEATHER FASCINATOR

[1] Scan or trace all the fascinator templates on page 122 and cut out. Cut the felt into two rectangles, 6 x 2½ inches (15 x 6.5 cm). Place one piece on top of the other and draw around the hair clip cover template with an air-erasable pen. Using thread to match the felt, machine sew around the marked shape to join the layers, leaving the flat end of the shape open and long thread ends at the beginning and end of the stitches.

[2] Push the awl through the dots on the hair clip cover template to mark them with holes. Place the paper template on one side of the felt piece, within the stitch line, and mark through the holes, using a white marker pen to transfer the dots to the felt. Cut a slot between the dots through one layer of felt only. Snap open the clip and slide it into the felt pocket, being careful to push the back of the clip only out through the slot.

[3] Pull the excess thread ends through to one side and use them to hand sew a running stitch around the open end. Trim the excess felt to within ⅟₃₂–⅟₁₆ inch (1–1.5 mm) of the stitch line.

[4] Using a black ballpoint pen, draw around the paper template for the leather part of the fascinator to transfer the outline to the front of the piece of leather. Mark all the dots through into the leather using the awl. The six dots near the top of the petals mark the positions of the brads—use the punch to make only a very small hole through these dots.

[5] With the same thread used for sewing the felt, sew back and then forth again to make a double line of sewing between the punched hole and the awl hole on each petal shape. Trim excess threads.

[6] Punch out two ³⁄₁₆-inch (5-mm) holes over the dots at the bottom of the leather shape and set a ³⁄₁₆-inch (5-mm) eyelet in each. Carefully cut out the leather shape.

[7] Using the permanent marker, draw around the paper template for the plastic/fabric part of the fascinator to transfer the shape to the square of plastic, including the lines between the scallops. Cut around only the outline of the shape.

[8] Gripping the feathers on the trim near the tape, pull out four clumps of feathers of about four feathers in each, a large one at the back with smaller ones on top, ascending in length.

[9] Turn the plastic shape over and place the feathers right side down onto it—with the smallest feathers nearest the plastic and the biggest on top—aligning the quills with the lines between the scallops drawn on the reverse of the plastic. Machine stitch the feathers onto the plastic with zigzag stitches over the quills until secure.

[10] Turn the plastic shape over again, so that the quills are now concealed underneath, and the decorative part of the feather shows over the top edge.

Sew the feathers in securely at the bottom to stop them from moving around and getting ragged or damaged while you complete the project.

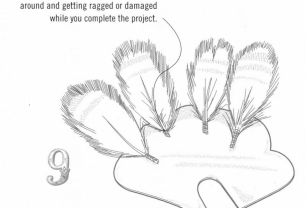

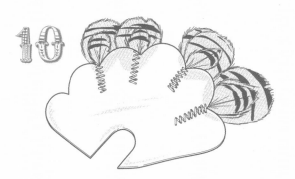

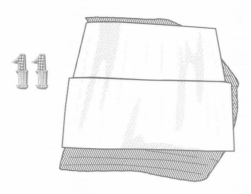

[11] Attach two strips of double-sided tape across the back of the square of herringbone fabric. Turn the plastic/fabric paper template over to reverse it and draw around it onto the paper backing of the tape, using the permanent marker. Cut out the shape.

[12] Peel off one of the paper backing strips and secure the fabric to the front of the plastic shape, aligning the edges of the fabric with the edges of the plastic. Peel off the second strip of backing paper and smooth the remaining section of fabric down. Using beige thread and a small zigzag stitch, machine sew all the way around the edge of the plastic/fabric shape.

[13] Place the paper template over the plastic/fabric shape and transfer the dots marking the position of the brads, using the awl. Use the punch to make the holes in the plastic/fabric shape large enough to take the brads.

[14] Lay the leather piece on top of the fabric side of the plastic/fabric shape and push one brad through each hole to join together all the layers, opening the arms of each brad out on the back.

Make sure you replace the sewing machine needle after sewing together the plastic and fabric, because glue from the tape will be stuck to it.

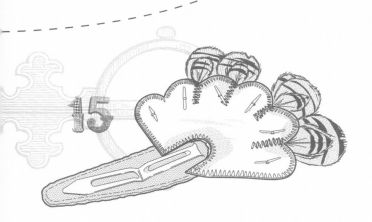

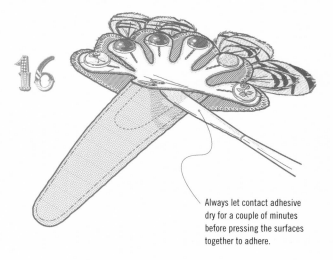

Always let contact adhesive dry for a couple of minutes before pressing the surfaces together to adhere.

[15] Slide the closed end of the felt-covered hair clip between the fabric and leather layers at the bottom of the piece and use the air-erasable pen to mark the felt along the edge of the fabric/plastic shape where it overlaps the back of the clip. Remove the clip and spread a thin layer of solvent-based contact adhesive on the back of the felt within the marked line and on the front of the fabric, being careful not to get any on the leather. Let the adhesive dry for a minute or two, then secure the felt and fabric together.

[16] Turn the piece over and use the air-erasable pen to mark the felt along the edge of the leather where it rests on top of the clip. Avoiding the eyelet area, spread a thin layer of contact adhesive on top of the felt within the marked line and on the back of the leather. Let the adhesive dry for a minute or two, then secure the leather to the felt.

[17] Punch a ³⁄₁₆-inch (5-mm) hole through both layers of felt, avoiding the metal of the clip inside, and set a ³⁄₁₆-inch (5-mm) eyelet. Using green embroidery floss and starting on the back of the clip, sew the point of the leather down through the eyelets and the two layers of felt as shown and knot off on the back.

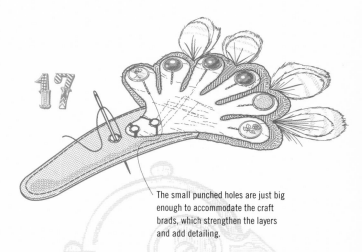

The small punched holes are just big enough to accommodate the craft brads, which strengthen the layers and add detailing.

HAT COCKADE

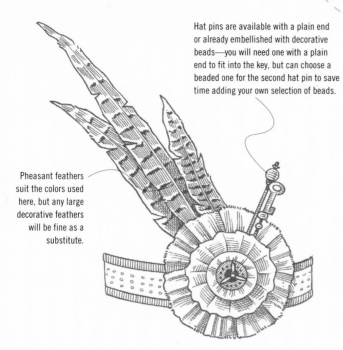

Hat pins are available with a plain end or already embellished with decorative beads—you will need one with a plain end to fit into the key, but can choose a beaded one for the second hat pin to save time adding your own selection of beads.

Pheasant feathers suit the colors used here, but any large decorative feathers will be fine as a substitute.

YOU WILL NEED

- Brass pierced clock cog, about 1 in. (25 mm) diameter
- Pocket watch face, about 1½ in. (40 mm) diameter
- Single-hole dark red flat button with the back loop removed
- Small brass propeller
- Brass flower bead cap, flattened with hammer
- Antique gold head pin
- 20-in. (50-cm) length of 1 in. (25 mm) dark red grosgrain ribbon
- Dark red and black sewing thread
- Piece of red felt, 2½ in. (6.5 cm) square
- Strip of traditional cream-and-blue striped mattress ticking, 2 x 40 in. (5 x 100 cm)
- Cream topstitching thread
- Piece of white felt, 4 in. (10 cm) square
- Black bowler hat
- 28-in. (70-cm) length of 1⅜ in. (35 mm) wine-red velvet ribbon

- 28-in. (70-cm) length of 1 in. (25 mm) black-and-gold polka dot grosgrain ribbon
- 3 pheasant feathers
- Small selection of seed beads in different sizes
- 2 gold hat pins
- Small metal key
- 4 antique brass 5 mm bead caps
- 2 round pearl beads in different sizes
- Copper 5 mm rondelle spacer bead
- 3 burgundy small round glass beads
- 2 small brass watch cogs, about 1 in. (25 mm) diameter
- Brass ³⁄₁₆ in. (5 mm) tube/washer bead
- Superglue gel
- Hammer
- Wire cutters
- Round-nose pliers
- Metal ruler
- Black ballpoint pen
- Hand sewing needle
- Scissors
- Sewing machine
- Iron
- Pins
- Leather punch
- Flat-nose pliers or a thimble
- Small metal file

COMPLETE YOUR STEAMPUNK OUTFIT with this fabulous feathered bowler—just the thing to make an entrance at a special event or for an unforgettable night on the town. The cockade is easy to make—but you could cheat and just add the watch face section to a purchased rosette for a fast result.

HOW TO MAKE THE HAT COCKADE

COCKADE

[1] Glue the watch cog onto the front of the pocket watch face with dabs of superglue gel, then add the button, propeller, and flattened bead cap. Let dry.

[2] Thread the head pin through the center of the watch/cog assembly. Cut it down to ⅝ inch (1.5 mm), then use round-nose pliers to curl the wire end into a loop tight against the back.

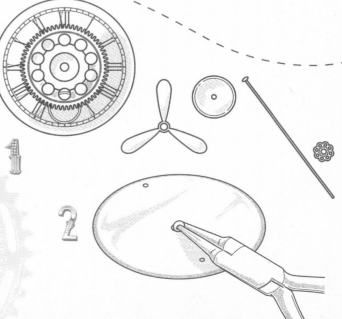

[3] Starting 1½ inches (40 mm) from one end, make a mark at every ¼ inch (6 mm) along the edge of the red grosgrain ribbon, using the ballpoint pen.

[4] Thread the hand sewing needle with a doubled length of dark red thread and knot the ends. Fold the ribbon back on the first mark and make a stitch in the side of the ribbon near the mark, then pass the needle between the two strands of thread and pull tight to secure.

[5] Count five marks down the ribbon, then pinch and fold the ribbon at the fifth mark.

[6] Bring the fold over to align with the next mark along from the stitch made in step 4. Sew from back to front through the top three layers of ribbon. Make a second stitch in the same place, again passing the needle between the two strands of thread to make a knot.

[7] Repeat steps 5 and 6 until you have made fourteen pleats. Join the pleats into a circle.

[8] With right sides together, sew across the ends of the ribbon at the back, just after the last pleat. Trim the ribbon ends, leaving a ½-inch (10-mm) seam allowance.

[9] Run a tiny amount of superglue down the edge of the ribbon to stop it fraying. Let dry. Fold over the seam allowance and sew down to the back of the ribbon rosette, pulling the tip at the outside edge down a little before sewing so that it doesn't show above the edge on the right side. Be careful that the stitches do not show on the front.

[10] Draw a 2-inch (50-mm) diameter circle on the red felt with the ballpoint pen. Draw a 1-inch (25-mm) diameter circle in the center of the bigger circle. Cut out the felt around the outer line.

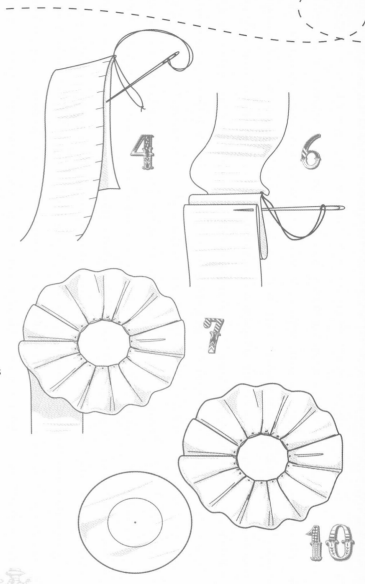

❀ **Note:** If your ticking has wider stripes than those shown here, you can adjust the box pleats to match the stripes. This may mean that the center of the rosette will not fit neatly onto the 1½-inch (40-mm) diameter circle on the white felt; this does not matter because it is just a guideline and will be hidden by the red rosette.

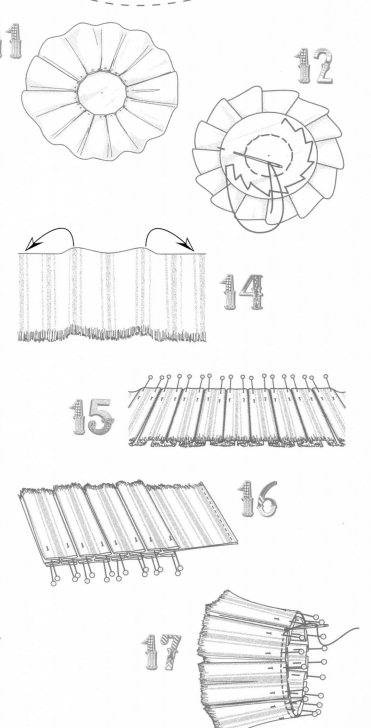

[11] Place the rosette on the felt circle and sew the inside edge of the rosette to the felt inner circle line, just catching the edge of each fold and arranging the pleats evenly.

[12] Turn over the rosette and hand sew the back folds of the loops of ribbon to the felt, making sure that the stitches do not show on the front of the rosette. Turn the rosette over again and iron it flat on the wrong side.

[13] Rip a raw edge down one long side of the ticking. Trim the other side to make a strip about 1¼ inches (30 mm) wide and 28 inches (70 cm) long.

[14] Working along the neater edge of the strip, fold along the middle of one of the stripes, then bring the fold over to the right to meet the middle of the second stripe to the right. Pin in place. Skip one stripe to the left of the fold, then fold over the next stripe along to meet the second stripe on the left in the same way. Pin in place.

[15] Continue in this way until you have made nine box pleats, with the folds on each side of each pleat just touching. Mark the stripe below the last fold at each end, then remove the final pin at each end.

[16] Fold over the pleated section, right sides together, and sew across to join the marked stripes. Trim the seam allowance to ³⁄₁₆ inch (5 mm).

[17] Turn the tube the right side out and hand sew through all the layers to sew the pleats together along the cut edge only, using the cream topstitching thread.

[18] Flatten the rosette and press gently.

[19] Draw a 3-inch (7.5-cm) circle on the white felt with the ballpoint pen. Draw another 1½-inch (40-mm) diameter circle in the center of the bigger circle. Cut out the felt around the outer line. Place the ticking rosette on the white felt circle and sew the inside edge of the ticking rosette to the felt inner circle line, just catching the edge of each fold and arranging the pleats evenly. Turn over and sew the back pleats to the back edge of the felt, making sure the stitches do not show on the front of the rosette, and iron it flat.

[20] Sew the red rosette on top of the ticking rosette around the edge of the red felt center, using a running stitch. Punch a small hole in the center of the red felt circle, through all layers, to take the loop on the back of the watch face. Push the loop through the hole, then set the finished cockade aside.

HAT RIBBONS
[21] Remove the existing ribbon from the bowler hat.

[22] Tightly pin the velvet ribbon around the hat. Remove the ribbon and place the ribbon ends right sides together. Sew across at the pin mark, then trim the seam allowance to 3/16 inch (5 mm). Slide the ribbon back onto the hat, placing the ribbon's seam on the right, toward the front of the hat.

[23] Repeat step 22, using the narrower polka dot ribbon on top of the velvet ribbon. Use the curved end of a metal ruler to lift and slide the polka dot ribbon over the velvet ribbon, lining up the seams.

[24] Roll out the band inside the hat. Using black thread, hand sew through the top and bottom edges of the polka dot ribbon into the hat, at the front seam, center back, and on each side of the hat to secure the ribbons. Replace the band.

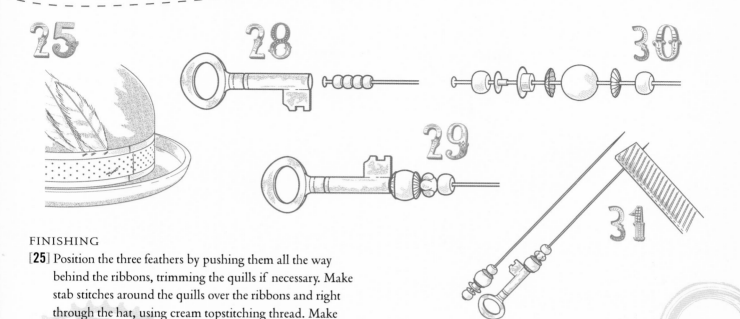

FINISHING

[25] Position the three feathers by pushing them all the way behind the ribbons, trimming the quills if necessary. Make stab stitches around the quills over the ribbons and right through the hat, using cream topstitching thread. Make two sets of stitches, one just below the top edge of ribbons and one near the bottom edge. Knot the thread ends inside.

[26] Thread a needle with doubled cream topstitching thread and knot the ends. Push the needle from the inside out through the hat to where the center of the cockade will lie. Thread the needle through the loop on the back of the pocket watch and back inside the hat, next to where the thread came out, between the two strands of threads, and pull tight to secure. Tie the thread in a knot, then carry on making stab stitches to sew the red felt to the hat with small hidden stitches. You will need to use pliers or a thimble to get the needle through the hat.

[27] Make stab stitches to sew the ticking onto the hat, hiding the stitches inside the pleats.

[28] Thread a few seed beads onto one of the hat pins, then push the head of the hat pin inside the key shaft to work out which size and how many seed beads fit snugly inside the key shaft to hold the hat pin in place. Glue the beads and hat pin into the key shaft, using superglue gel.

[29] Thread a bead cap, pearl, bead cap, rondelle spacer bead, and small glass bead onto the bottom of the hat pin. Pull back the last bead, add a dab of superglue to the pin above it, then push the bead back over the glue and up next to the other beads. Let dry.

[30] Thread a selection of cogs and beads onto the other hat pin. Pull back the last bead as before, add a dab of superglue to the pin above it, then slide the bead back over the glue and let dry.

[31] Push the hat pins into the hat to see if either one needs shortening. If it does, remove and cut the pin to the desired length with wire cutters. File the end back into a point with the metal file.

[32] Push the hat pins back into the hat. When they are in the correct position, pull each one out a little and put a tiny dab of superglue on the pin right next to the fabric of the hat. Push the hat pins back in and let dry.

OCULUS GOGGLES

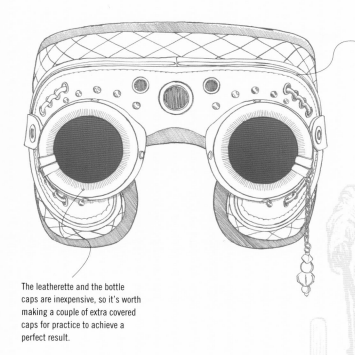

Cutting on the bias means that the longer measurement is set out at a diagonal across the fabric. This makes the strips of leatherette very stretchy.

Note: See pages 126–127 for the goggles templates. Don't be put off by the lengthy list of materials required—one session at an online craft store (or a visit to your local crafts retailer) should net you everything you need.

The leatherette and the bottle caps are inexpensive, so it's worth making a couple of extra covered caps for practice to achieve a perfect result.

UNCOMPROMISINGLY STEAMPUNK in appearance, these goggles have been designed around the 3-D glasses you use for movies (for the more discreet enthusiast, you can don them when the lights go down). If you're brave in your approach, however, a little modification will make them useful as sunglasses or even reading glasses! The only requirement is that the lenses you use should be round and fairly small.

❖ YOU WILL NEED

- ❖ 2 plastic screw caps, 1½ in. (40 mm) diameter
- ❖ Piece of antique bronze leatherette, 10 x 54 in. (25 x 140 cm)
- ❖ Bronze, olive-green, and dark red sewing thread
- ❖ 2 plastic 1-quart (2.27-liter) milk or juice bottles/cartons
- ❖ 40-in. (1-m) length of ¹⁄₁₆ in. (1.5 mm) smooth piping cord
- ❖ Bronze topstitching thread
- ❖ 16 new and antique copper ⅛ in. (3 mm) eyelets
- ❖ 1 black ⁵⁄₁₆ in. (8 mm) eyelet, rubbed with fine sandpaper
- ❖ 5 antique copper ³⁄₁₆ in. (5 mm) eyelets
- ❖ 5 antique copper 9 mm nipple-head

- jean rivets
- ❖ 2 metallic bronze ¼ in. (6 mm) cupped sequins
- ❖ 35 metallic copper mini craft brads
- ❖ Scrap of brown leather
- ❖ 2 gold metal sliders, rubbed with fine sandpaper
- ❖ 20-in. (50-cm) length of dark red plush finishing elastic
- ❖ Pair of 3-D glasses or flat lensed sunglasses
- ❖ Piece of sage-green velvet, 8 x 12 in. (20 x 30 cm)
- ❖ Piece of white cotton double-sided quilted fabric, 8 x 12 in. (20 x 30 cm)
- ❖ 40-in. (1-m) length of ½ in. (10 mm) sage-green cotton bias binding

- ❖ 40-in. (1-m) length of round turquoise leather cord
- ❖ 22-in. (55-cm) length of antique gold medium curb chain
- ❖ Light green small glass bicone bead
- ❖ Lilac small round glass bead
- ❖ Light blue crystal bicone bead
- ❖ Emerald small faceted glass bead
- ❖ Size 11 green seed bead
- ❖ Antique gold eyepin
- ❖ Antique gold 8 mm jump ring
- ❖ Craft knife
- ❖ Medium (P80) and fine (P600) wet and dry sandpaper
- ❖ Metal ruler
- ❖ Pins
- ❖ Sewing machine with heavy needle options and zipper foot

- ❖ Sharp scissors
- ❖ Solvent-based contact adhesive
- ❖ Paper and scissors for templates
- ❖ Small sponge
- ❖ Black ballpoint pen
- ❖ Awl
- ❖ Leather punch
- ❖ Eyelet setting tool for ⅛ in. (3 mm), ³⁄₁₆ in. (5 mm), and ⁵⁄₁₆ in. (8 mm) eyelets
- ❖ Rivet setting tool
- ❖ Masking tape
- ❖ Fine permanent marking pen
- ❖ Air-erasable marking pen
- ❖ Hand sewing needle
- ❖ Small safety pin
- ❖ Wire cutters
- ❖ 2 pairs of small pliers

HOW TO MAKE THE OCULUS GOGGLES

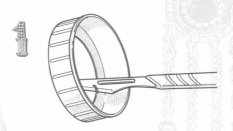

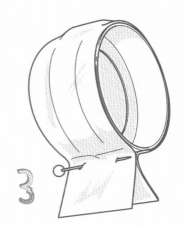

LEATHERETTE MASK

[1] Roughly cut out the very center of each plastic cap with a craft knife. Trim the edges to a neat 1¼-inch (30 mm) diameter in the center of the cap. Sand the caps lightly, inside and out.

[2] Cut two strips of leatherette on the bias, each about 1¼ inches (30 mm) wide by about 8 inches (20 cm) long.

[3] Pulling the leatherette strip slightly, pin it tightly around one lid. Unpin and transfer the pin mark measurement onto the second strip.

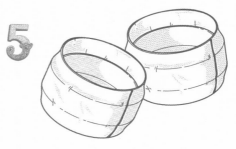

[4] With right sides together and using bronze thread, machine sew the strips into tubes. Trim the seam allowances to ⅛ inch (3 mm) and glue them down, using solvent-based contact adhesive. Turn the tubes the right sides out.

[5] Pull each tube over a cap, so that the cap sits in the center of the length of tube.

[6] Spread a thin layer of contact adhesive on the top edge of the lid, all over the inside of the rim, and on the inside surface of the leatherette, above the lid. Leave until tacky.

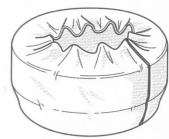

[7] Secure the leatherette to the cap, working from the outside edge in and trying to smooth out any wrinkles as you work.

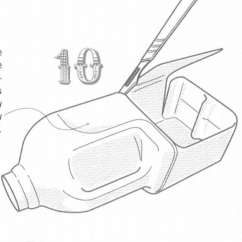

Many large milk or juice plastic bottles/cartons are made from HDPE (high-density polyethylene)—it is translucent and not usually colored, and it is both sturdy and easy to cut.

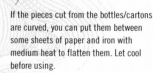

If the pieces cut from the bottles/cartons are curved, you can put them between some sheets of paper and iron with medium heat to flatten them. Let cool before using.

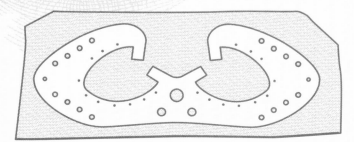

[8] Push the leatherette inside the cap and secure it to the underside of the rim.

[9] Now spread a thin layer of adhesive around the inside of the cap on the screw thread and on the inside of the exposed leatherette. Leave until tacky, then secure the leatherette inside the cap from the other end.

[10] Cut out the largest flat areas from the plastic bottles/cartons to get flat pieces big enough for one mask and two eye tube pieces.

[11] Scan or trace all the template pieces on pages 126–127 and cut out. Place the mask and eye tube templates on the pieces of plastic and trim the plastic roughly around the shapes, leaving a small allowance around the edges; cut one mask and two eye tubes.

[12] Lightly sand both sides of each piece of plastic with fine wet and dry sandpaper.

[13] Cut a piece of leatherette slightly larger than the mask and two pieces each slightly larger than the eye tubes. Spread a thin layer of solvent-based contact adhesive on one side of each piece of plastic and on the back of each piece of leatherette with a small piece of sponge. Let dry, then secure the pieces of leatherette to the corresponding pieces of plastic.

[14] Place the mask template on the right side of the leatherette/plastic piece and mark around the edge and in the holes with the ballpoint pen. Mark the dots through to the plastic, using the awl.

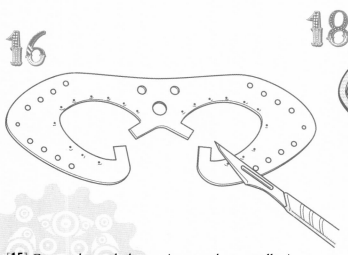

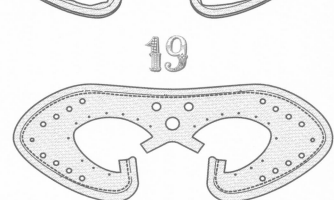

[15] Cut out the mask shape using very sharp, small scissors. Push the awl through all the marks (except the marks on the flaps near B and C) from front to back to make small holes for the brad fasteners. The marks near B and C are to indicate where to fold the flaps.

[16] Slice off any rough edges of plastic on the back, using the craft knife with the blade flat to the surface. Punch out the sixteen holes in four groups of four to take the ⅛-inch (3-mm) eyelets, the centered hole for the ⁵⁄₁₆-inch (8-mm) eyelet, the holes on each side of this for two ³⁄₁₆-inch (5-mm) eyelets, and the holes at each end for two 9-mm jean rivets.

[17] Cut a strip of leatherette 1 inch (25 mm) wide and 18 inches (46 cm) long. Fold it in half lengthwise, wrong sides together, laying the piping cord in the fold. Sew together the two layers as close to the cord as possible, using the zipper foot on the sewing machine.

[18] Lay the piping so it sits around the very edge of the mask, with the raw edges on the inside of the mask. Using solvent-based contact adhesive, glue the piping in place. Let dry.

[19] Using bronze topstitching thread, sew the piping onto the mask from the front, machine sewing around the mask ¹⁄₁₆ inch (1.5 mm) in from the edge. Sew back and forth at each end of the stitches to secure. Cut off the piping flush with the ends of the mask. On the back of the mask, trim away the excess seam allowance on the piping.

[20] Set the eyelets in the mask—the ⅛-inch (3-mm) eyelets in four groups of four, the centered ⁵⁄₁₆-inch (8-mm) eyelet, and the two ³⁄₁₆-inch (5-mm) eyelets on each side of the centered eyelet.

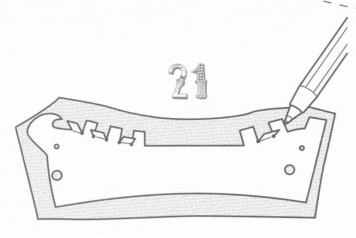

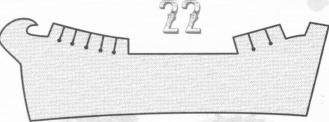

[21] Lay the eye tube template on the right side of the
leatherette/plastic. Fold back alternate flaps, then draw
around the template with the ballpoint pen, including
inside the four tabs. Mark all the dots through onto the
leatherette/plastic, using the awl.

[22] Cut out the eye tube with very sharp, small scissors,
cutting across the top of the two blocks of flaps as a
continuous line. Working from the front, punch through
the pairs of awl marks on each side for the jean rivet and
the eyelet, and the single mark in the curled tab for the
sequin/brad. Snip between the flaps, stopping at the brad
marks. Repeat steps 21 and 22 for the other eye tube,
remembering to turn over the template before drawing
around it.

[23] Roll the leatherette/plastic around into a tube, lining
up the holes for the jean rivet and eyelet. Set a jean rivet
into the smaller holes and a ³/₁₆-inch (5-mm) eyelet into
the larger holes.

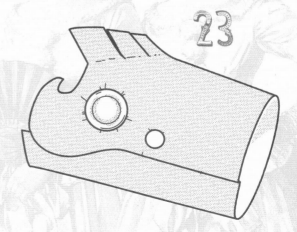

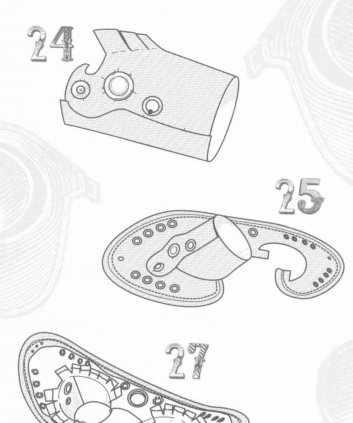

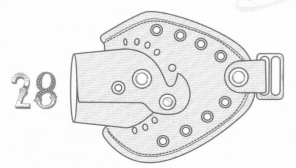

[24] Fit the sequins onto the curled tabs with a brad fastener through the hole. Fold all the flaps forward.

[25] Fold up the flaps on the mask, along the marks at B and C. Slot the right eye tube into the right side of the mask, tucking all the flaps in toward the back but leaving the curled tab with the sequin on top of the mask.

[26] Make sure the B flap on the mask is as close as possible to the section of three flaps on the eye tube. Starting at the hole marked D on the mask template, push the awl through the hole to make a matching mark on the flap below, as close as possible to the center of the flap. From the back, make a hole in the flap through the mark, using the awl. From the front of the mask, push a brad fastener through the hole and through the flap, and open out on the inside of the mask. Repeat in the same way for the other two holes next to hole D, then with the hole marked A and the six holes next to it.

[27] Push the awl through holes B and C on the eye tube template to make a corresponding mark onto the flap on the mask beneath. Make the marks into holes in the flap, as described in step 26. From the front of the eye tube, push a brad fastener through each hole, through the flap, and open out on the inside of the mask. On the inside of the mask, make sure all the brad arms are flat to the mask. Secure the left eye tube in the same way.

[28] Transfer the template for the loop onto the scrap of leather, cut out the shape, and punch out the holes. Thread one side bar of a slider onto the strip of leather and fold the strip in half, sliding the mask between the two layers and aligning the holes. Set a jean rivet through the holes to secure the loop in place. Repeat to fit another loop with slider on the other side of the mask.

[29] Cut a strip of leatherette twice the width of the finishing elastic and 3 inches (7.5 cm) long. Fold it over one end of the elastic, so that the long edges meet along the center back of the elastic, and glue in place with solvent-based contact adhesive.

[30] Sew around all sides of the leatherette as close as possible to the edges, using bronze topstitching thread. Thread one end through the slider on the left-hand side of the mask and fold over the last 1 inch (25 mm) to the inside. Punch a hole through both layers and set in a jean rivet to secure the elastic strap in place. Punch another hole for the 3⁄16 inch (5 mm) eyelet through the single thickness of leatherette-covered elastic and set in an eyelet.

[31] Put squares of masking tape on the lenses of the 3-D glasses and label "left" and "right" with an arrow to show which direction is up. Remove the lenses from the frames.

[32] Using the lenses template on page 127 and the permanent marker, mark and cut out circles from the centers of the lenses. Pop the lenses inside the leatherette-covered caps, then push the caps onto the ends of the eye tubes. Adjust until the seams on the leatherette coverings are symmetrical and the lenses are correctly oriented.

[33] Place a couple of fingers inside each eye tube, in turn, to offer support from the inside, and use the awl to make four holes in the side of each cap at the top, bottom, and equally on each side.

[34] Remove the caps again and use the awl to make corresponding holes around the end of each eye tube. Place the caps back on the eye tubes and secure each in place with four brad fasteners through the holes. Peel the masking tape off the lenses.

FABRIC MASK

[35] Pin the velvet, right side up, on top of the quilted fabric. Mark a diagonal line across the middle with the air-erasable pen, then machine sew down the line, using olive-green thread. Use the sewing machine foot as a guide to sew more lines parallel to the first and approximately ¼ inch (6 mm) apart.

[36] Mark a second line across the middle of the fabric at an angle to the first line and repeat the stitches, as in step 35, to create a quilted diamond pattern on the fabric.

[37] Pin the fabric mask template onto the right side of the patterned velvet. Draw around the edge with the air-erasable pen, then cut out the shape along the line.

[38] Open out the folds on the bias binding. With right sides together, pin, then machine sew, along one fold line to attach the bias binding to the fabric mask around the eye holes, around the bridge of the nose, and then around the outside edges. Fold the bias binding back over the raw edges of the mask to the back. Sew it to the back of the mask by hand, tucking and folding in the tape ends as you work.

ASSEMBLING THE GOGGLES

[39] Using the bronze topstitching thread doubled, hand sew the fabric mask to the leatherette mask by first sewing around flaps B and C and through to the back of the fabric.

[40] Now that the two layers are attached in the center, pin the sliders to the fabric mask so that it does not move around. Cut the leather cord in half and tie a knot in one end. Make a hole with the awl through the fabric mask from front to back near to the end eyelet in one of the groups of four. Thread the cord through the hole from the front, leaving the knot sandwiched between the fabric and leatherette masks, out of sight. Poke another hole through the fabric at the position of the end eyelet and thread the cord through to the front of the leatherette mask.

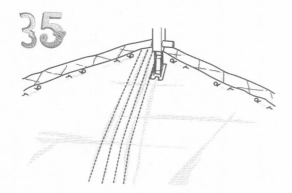

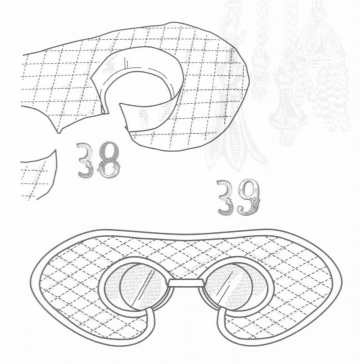

[41] Make another hole through the fabric through the next eyelet hole and thread the cord back through to the back. Make a second hole through the same eyelet, as far apart as possible from the first, and bring the cord back through to the front. Keep poking holes with the awl in the direction that you are sewing the cord in and out through the eyelets.

[42] At the fourth eyelet, bring the cord across the back of the fabric to the next group of four eyelets and repeat the sewing process. When you have finished sewing, knot the end of the cord so that it is hidden between two masks. Repeat on the other two groups of eyelets on the other side of the mask.

[43] Now try on the mask and thread the other end of the elastic through the slider on the right-hand side. Place a pin in the elastic to mark the correct length. Remove the mask, then sew across the elastic below the metal slider to secure in place, trimming off any excess and folding the raw end under before sewing.

[44] Support the mask on a large can or similar item. Make a small hole in the left eye tube just below the eyelet. Cut a 14-inch (35-cm) length of curb chain and find a point along it just off center; push the chain at this point through the eyelet. Push a brad fastener through the hole below the eyelet, from the front to the inside of the tube, then thread the arms of the brad through a link of the chain on the inside, and open the arms out.

[45] Using the small safety pin, temporarily attach the other ends of the chain to the eyelet in the strap. Thread the beads onto the eyepin, cut off the excess wire, and use round-nose pliers to curl the wire end into a loop. Using the wire cutters, cut one of the hanging loops of chain just down from the front of the mask and insert the beaded eyepin into the chain length. Cut two more lengths of chain measuring 1¾ inches (45 mm) and 2½ inches (65 mm) and add these to the safety pin. When you are happy with the effect, replace the safety pin with the jump ring.

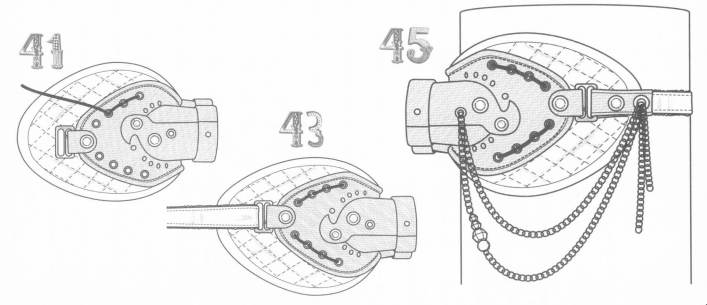

TEMPLATES

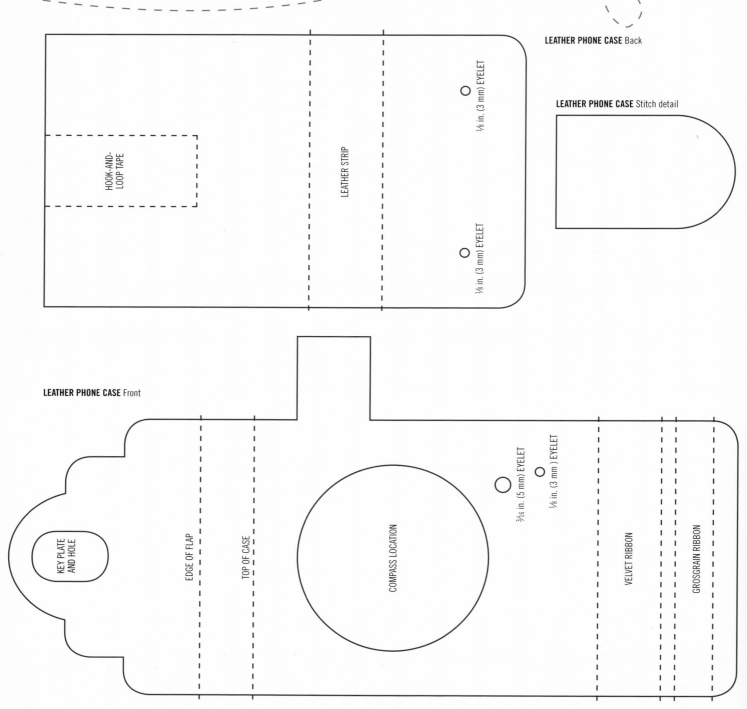

LEATHER PHONE CASE Back

HOOK-AND-LOOP TAPE

LEATHER STRIP

1/8 in. (3 mm) EYELET

1/8 in. (3 mm) EYELET

LEATHER PHONE CASE Stitch detail

LEATHER PHONE CASE Front

KEY PLATE AND HOLE

EDGE OF FLAP

TOP OF CASE

COMPASS LOCATION

3/16 in. (5 mm) EYELET

1/8 in. (3 mm) EYELET

VELVET RIBBON

GROSGRAIN RIBBON

LEATHER PHONE CASE
Flap lining

HOOK-AND-LOOP TAPE

LEATHER PHONE CASE Background image

LEATHER PHONE CASE
Compass image

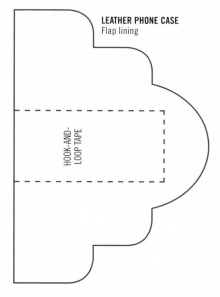

CANISTER CASE Numbers

121

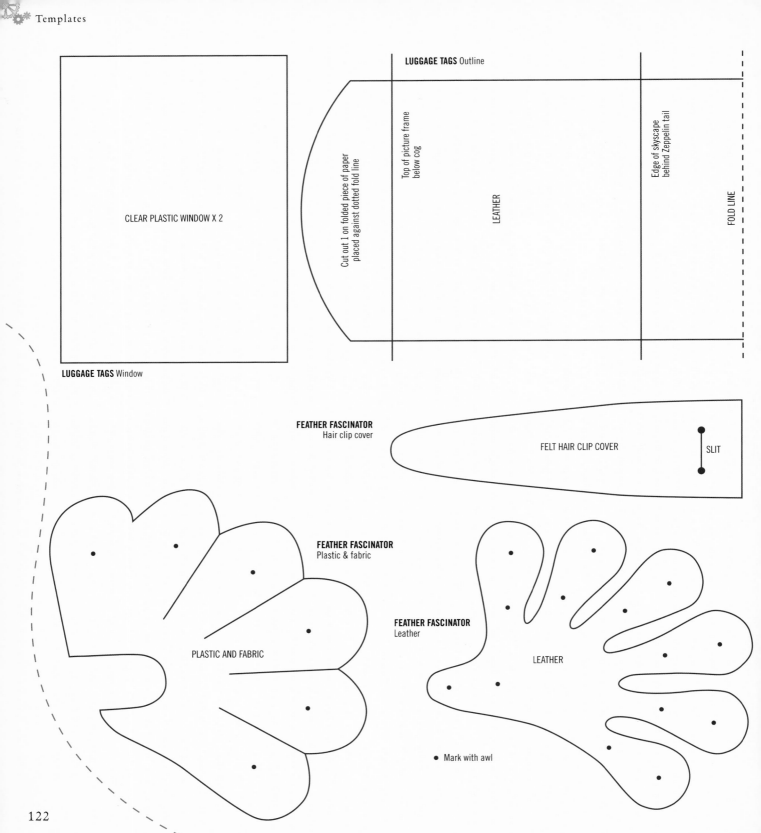

CLEAR PLASTIC WINDOW X 2

LUGGAGE TAGS Outline

Cut out 1 on folded piece of paper placed against dotted fold line

Top of picture frame below cog

LEATHER

Edge of skyscape behind Zeppelin tail

FOLD LINE

LUGGAGE TAGS Window

FEATHER FASCINATOR
Hair clip cover

FELT HAIR CLIP COVER

SLIT

FEATHER FASCINATOR
Plastic & fabric

PLASTIC AND FABRIC

FEATHER FASCINATOR
Leather

LEATHER

• Mark with awl

LUGGAGE TAGS Oval frame image

LUGGAGE TAGS Zeppelin image

BOOT LIVERIES Ornament

PUNCHED HOLES

¼ in. (4 mm)
EYELET HOLE

LEATHER BELT

HIS & HERS BRACELETS

PLASTIC

VINTAGE BILLFOLD

Right-hand top corner of billfold front

Cut a rectangle of paper 3½ in. x 8½ in. (9 cm x 21 cm) and mark on it these punched holes

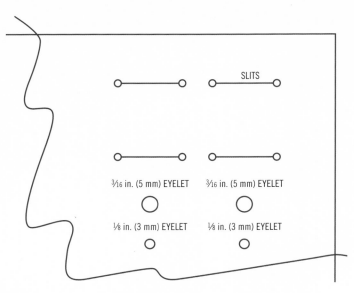

SLITS

³⁄₁₆ in. (5 mm) EYELET ³⁄₁₆ in. (5 mm) EYELET

⅛ in. (3 mm) EYELET ⅛ in. (3 mm) EYELET

VINTAGE BILLFOLD Typewriter keys image

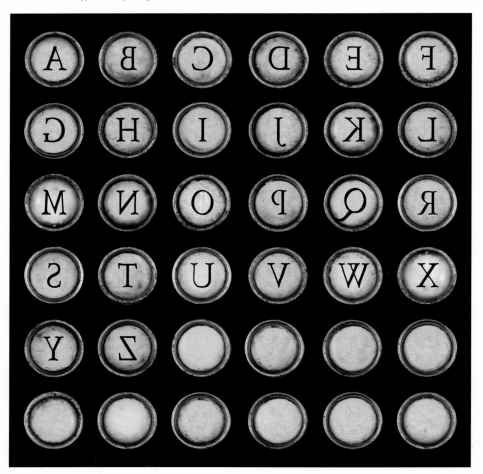

VINTAGE BILLFOLD
Top edge

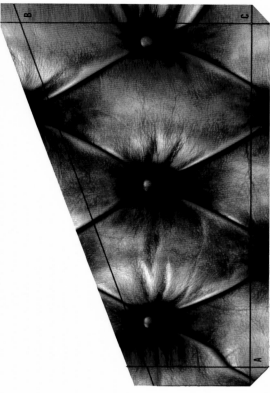

VINTAGE BILLFOLD
Pocket

VINTAGE BILLFOLD Behind pockets

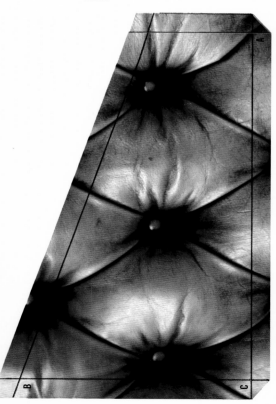

POCKET GAUNTLETS Cuff

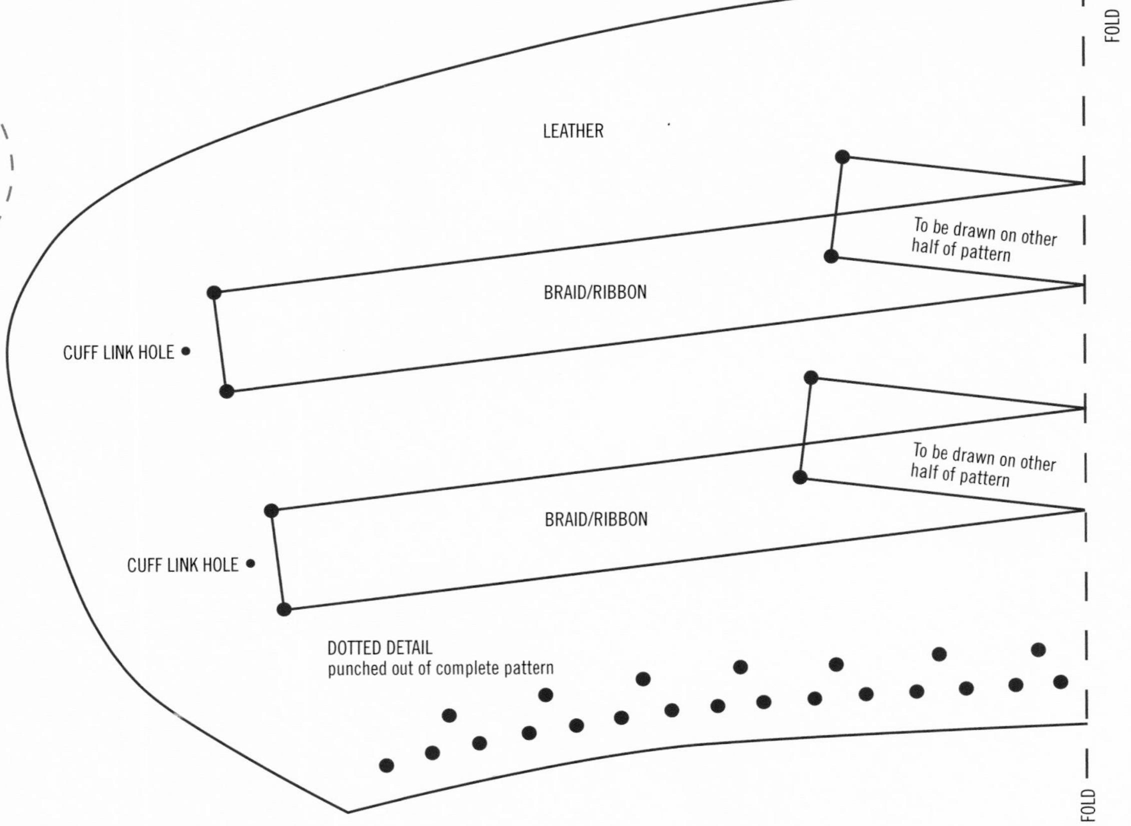

FOLD

LEATHER

To be drawn on other half of pattern

BRAID/RIBBON

CUFF LINK HOLE •

To be drawn on other half of pattern

BRAID/RIBBON

CUFF LINK HOLE •

DOTTED DETAIL
punched out of complete pattern

FOLD

● Punched holes in pattern

• To be marked with awl

POCKET GAUNTLETS Monocle pocket

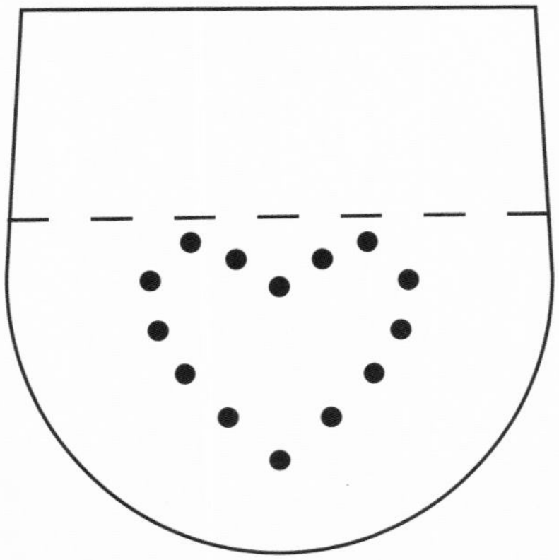

OCULUS GOGGLES
Leatherette/plastic mask

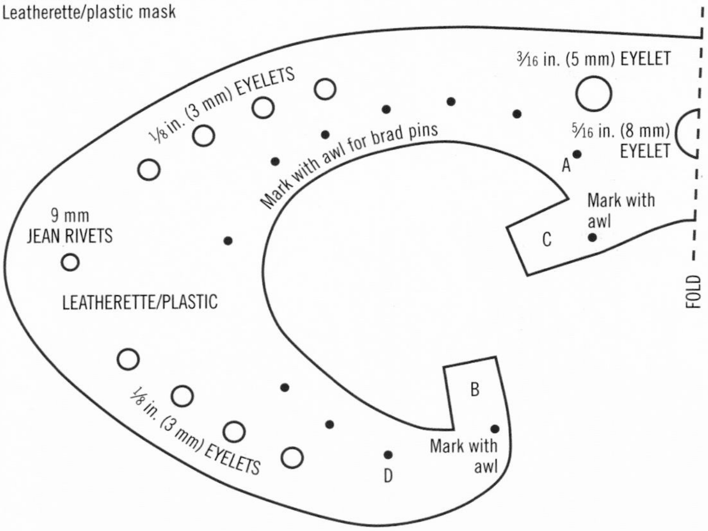

⅛ in. (3 mm) EYELETS

3⁄16 in. (5 mm) EYELET

Mark with awl for brad pins

5⁄16 in. (8 mm) EYELET

A

9 mm
JEAN RIVETS

Mark with awl

C

LEATHERETTE/PLASTIC

FOLD

⅛ in. (3 mm) EYELETS

B

Mark with awl

D

126

OCULUS GOGGLES Fabric mask

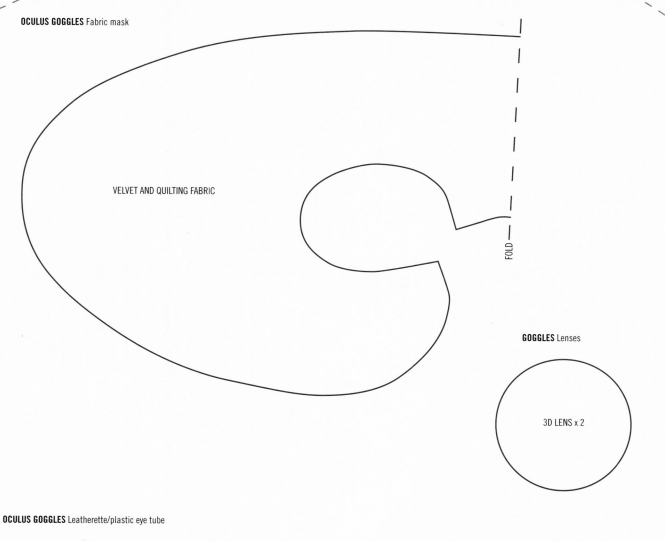

VELVET AND QUILTING FABRIC

FOLD

GOGGLES Lenses

3D LENS x 2

OCULUS GOGGLES Leatherette/plastic eye tube

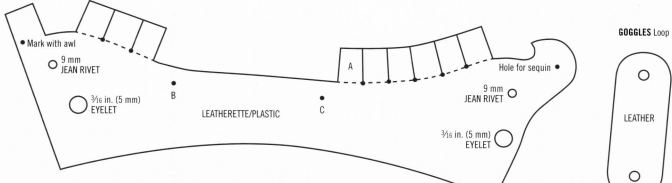

- Mark with awl

9 mm
JEAN RIVET

³⁄₁₆ in. (5 mm)
EYELET

B

A

C

LEATHERETTE/PLASTIC

Hole for sequin

9 mm
JEAN RIVET

³⁄₁₆ in. (5 mm)
EYELET

GOGGLES Loop

LEATHER

INDEX

Acknowledgments

Ivy Press would like to thank the following for generously supplying costumes and props:
- Darcy Clothing (Lewes)
- Brighton and Lewes Flea Markets

For permission to photograph on their premises:
- Lewes Forge
- The Mesmerist (Brighton)
- Brede Steam Engine Society
- The Smugglers Rest (Peacehaven)